CLARA CAKES

DELICIOUS AND SIMPLE VEGAN DESSERTS FOR EVERYONE

pH powerHouse Books
Brooklyn, NY

CLARA POLITO

To my mom for supporting
me from day one. If it weren't
for your constant love and
patience I wouldn't be writing
a book today. I wouldn't be
myself today. The past seven
years you've been watching
this book come to life. The past
nineteen years you've been
my best friend. Thank you
for providing me with endless
encouragement, advice, dance
breaks, and laughs.

Dessert Haikus
by Sophia Longo

TABLE OF CONTENTS

like everything else
good in life, cookies made with
love never crumble

under 21?
you can still enjoy bars on
the weekends—so sweet!

channeling pudding
right now on this dance floor—
tryna get saucy

breakfast, lunch, dinner
no rest, I'm always taking
my piece of the pie

icing my haters
watch out when my timer sounds
imma take the cake

hey wassup cutie?
I know u want to take a
lil' taste of this cake ;)

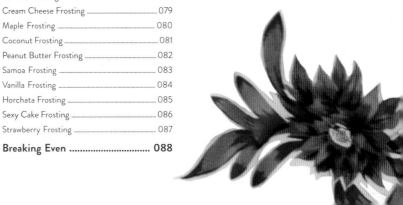

INTRODUCTION

In 2011, against our better judgment, my wife Deanna and I dragged ourselves up to the FYF Fest in Los Angeles. Our friends No Age were playing—and put us on their list—so it was kind of a no-brainer. Even if we did have to endure the traffic, the parking, and the lines to get in, we felt that the delivery would be worth the load. (It was.) No Age started as the sun hung low in the sky, sending a sheet of golden light out onto the faces of the crowd. I found myself in the space between the stage and the throngs of sweaty teenagers barely held back by a thick metal barrier. A few songs in, my focus shifted from the band to the hot-summer-wet, writhing ball of humanity watching them, bouncing and undulating with the music like a slimy box of live worms. Periodically one would pop up to the top and be tossed about on a sea of groping hands before waterfalling into the pit, where a couple of security humans would escort them out the side and they would immediately loop back into the wriggling mass of minions for another go. I was plucking photographic details out of a crowd that was acting out all the tropes of the modern concert experience. Smoking teens smashed against the gate by the circular dancing of dusty kids behind them, one fan dutifully mouthed the words to the songs while flailing his arms, another flipped me the bird, delivering the rebellious adolescent angst advertised. Among this scene I noticed two teenage girls, eyes on the stage as if the heavens were parting before them, jaws slack in awe and anticipation. I slid over and framed them in my tiny rectangle and pressed my shutter, freezing their faces from that millisecond of time onto a piece of film. Just another moment captured to wither away in my archive.

I soon found out that those two girls were Clara and her friend Sophia. I saw Clara talking through the fence to Randy Randall from No Age after the show, so I went up to weasel my way into their conversation, as one sometimes does. I discovered that she was a vegan baker who made delicious vegan cupcakes. This was of particular interest to me because I am a vegan who loves to eat delicious cupcakes. As we learned more about this lovely young woman, Deanna realized that she had read about Clara via quarrygirl's popular Instagram page. Quarrygirl posts reviews and promotions of vegan food, people, and products worldwide. There may have even been a photo of Clara's cream-filled cupcakes or her "Inception" cookies, which are an Oreo cookie baked into a chocolate chip cookie. Like letting a child choose their clothes for the day—of course they choose their Halloween

costume—these decadent sweets, with extra frosting or cookies injected into them, are what happens when a 13-year-old with an incurable sweet tooth makes dessert.

Clara's cakes were soon on everyone in my community's radar. Any cool art opening or concert wasn't complete without having Clara bring her cupcakes. I imagine this eighth grader rushing home from school in a frenzy, skirt rippling in the wind behind her like the wicked witch of the west, ghost-riding her bike like a scud missile into the front lawn, and running into mom's kitchen to fire up the oven and bake a few dozen cupcakes for a gig at the Smell that night. Still in her school uniform, lips perfectly painted in an impossibly red coat of glossy lipstick, sweat beading on her brow as she piles the frosting high with a well-coiffed

curl, homework be damned. I'm probably wrong about this. Do kids even wear uniforms or ride bikes to school in LA?

Clara is the kind of girl that gives me hope for future generations. She didn't wait for anything to happen to her, she made it happen for herself. With her incredibly cool and supportive mother as her backup, she has created the life she wants to live, and does the things she loves to do, and has already turned her passions into a viable career before leaving high school. If the creativity I have seen in her is any indication, I'm sure this book will be an instant classic: inventive, fun, and a great starting point and inspiration for young adults out there looking to carve their own path.

—Ed Templeton

A LOVE LETTER TO BAKING

I met you when I was 12. I don't know what it is about you, exactly, that I love. Maybe it's the comfort of knowing that if I follow your specific steps and measurements, I'll get one correct result. Forever and ever. It doesn't matter if I move to a new city, or if I'm having a bad day, or if I'm feeling lazy. As long as I follow the recipe, step by step, it'll come out the way it's supposed to.

From an outside perspective, you might seem like a very meticulous job or hobby to have. I have to follow your instructions word for word, double check that I add all the ingredients in all the right quantities, and wait patiently for our experiment to bake. You should be my worst nightmare. I can't focus on just one thing, be it a career or a baking step. I don't like math all that much, and I'm the furthest thing from a delicate, patient, pastry chef. It's inevitable that I'll knock something like cocoa powder all over the floor, especially if I'm crunched for time. I'm sloppy. I'm impatient. I want instant gratification. My hands are too shaky to do intricate decorating. I am everything a baker is not. Somehow, though, we managed to find each other and things just kinda worked.

When we met, a lot of things in my life were a bit unstable. I grew up moving around a lot.

I was in the seventh grade, freshly vegan and extra feisty about my newly found political beliefs and code of ethics. I was a stick. I could eat all the experiments we would come up with together and not stress out. I'd run it off in P.E. the next morning. I'd go to school, enjoy my friends and classes there, and walk home from school straight to you. I'd already have a plan of what we were gonna make together. At first it would be cookies and brownies. Then we'd gradually work our way up to cakes and pastries.

When it came time for me to graduate middle school, we had done a lot of fun things together. We found a niche for ourselves setting up shop at punk shows, selling out just in time to watch one of my favorite bands play. We had gotten customers, a couple magazine articles and blog posts written about us here and there, even an early morning news program that featured us. We made friends, a lot of new friends. In a way, I was just entering this whole new world you helped build for me.

Literally the day I graduated from middle school, my mom and I moved to a small apartment in LA. I ate dinner in my new, empty bedroom, looking at a distant view of the Hollywood sign. Everything felt a little uncertain in my life at that point. Money was

a huge concern, starting a brand new high school was scary, and we were leaving our family and friends behind. The feeling was all too familiar.

I started high school, and left within a month and did independent study instead. I told you, I wasn't good at focusing on one thing. It was my way of being able to pursue you. But as I said earlier, I'm really impatient. Things didn't really go full speed ahead. My dream was to open a shop, while still being a teenager, but I realized that you need a couple things called capital and credit to make that happen. Becoming an adult in LA, I started to realize that a working-class kid has to take about ten steps for every one stride an upper-class peer takes.

So we took those ten steps together. We doubled up on school work, started to bake cupcakes twice a week for a few different shops, and continued to sell at shows.

Eventually we'd be able to sell at music festivals, even beer festivals. We'd gain more customers, more friends, more recognition from all over the world. We'd design fun merch with artists we loved and ship them across the world. We'd do all that and then come home and bake, like exactly how it started.

You are my high school sweetheart, and as I'm writing this book, I realize that you are now my baby. I gave up things like a high school experience, and college, for us to be together—but I can't imagine life any other way. You were my best friend when I was feeling lonely. You were there to comfort me when I was heartbroken. You were there to empower me. You taught me the ropes of how a business works. You even taught me how to dance. Most of all, you've taught me how to be me.

xoxo, Clara

HOW THIS BOOK WORKS

I'm so honored that you bought my book! It's wild to imagine this book on shelves or sprawled out in kitchens that aren't mine. Thanks for inviting me in. In order to help us get to know each other and get baking, I wanna mention a few things that will make using this book and preparing these recipes much easier.

First off, every recipe in this book is vegan. I'm vegan, which is what encouraged me to start baking! Don't worry—baking without animal products is much easier than your parents might make it out to be! To help you make the transition I've got a big section of vegan substitutes listed in the back (in recipes, v. = vegan). Some items might need to be bought in advance from specialty stores, but most are readily available. When you're making your way through the book and something doesn't make sense, or you're not sure what to buy, check the back of the book for tips on what products you should look for or can use as substitutes.

You'll find additional tips and tricks throughout the book. Pretend it's my voice in the back of your mind helping you make it to sweet, sweet success.

Next, this is Clara Cakes, so you know the cakes are the star of the show. But before you dive into the cake section, check out my guide to constructing cupcakes and cakes at the beginning of that chapter. This is gonna help you prevent having a crumbled cake catastrophe! Every cake recipe will make 12 cupcakes, or one 9-inch round cake layer. If you want to make a two-layer cake, you'll need to double the recipe. If you need to

make a three-layer cake, you'll need to triple the recipe. Each frosting recipe will make enough to frost a dozen cupcakes or one cake layer. If you need to frost a two-layer cake, with a different filling, you'll need to double it. If making a two-layer cake with the same frosting for both the filling and frosting, you'll need to triple the recipe. Make sense?

While I've included my personal favorite cake, filling, and frosting combos in the cake section, all the recipes for the fillings and frostings are also listed separately. When you feel you have mastered the recipes I encourage you to experiment with mixing and matching cakes, frostings, and fillings to meet your own personal preferences

Most of all, welcome imperfection with open arms. If you're just starting to bake, you might screw up. It took me endless batches of sweets to figure out how to manipulate a list of ingredients into something delicious. If a dessert doesn't come out looking elegant, know that's not the goal of this book. The goal of this book is to show you how to make sweets that you crave the vegan way, that are even more satisfying than the non-vegan norm.

You have my book, now it's your time to make it feel like yours. Get batter, cocoa powder, and oil stains on it. That's what I would do. I hope you love this book, I hope your friends and family love this book, and I hope that it makes baking vegan seem a lot more approachable than it's made out to be. Let's do this!

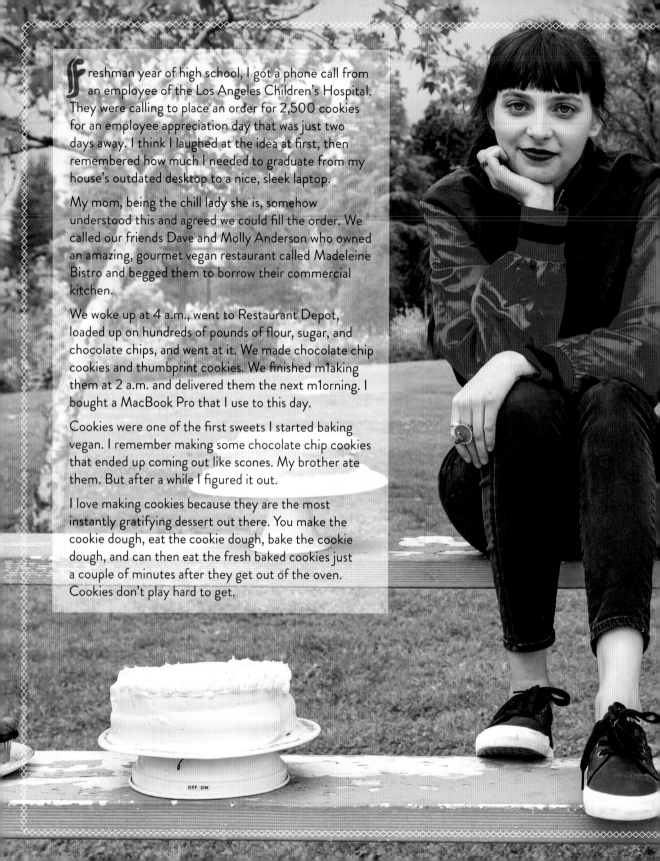

reshman year of high school, I got a phone call from an employee of the Los Angeles Children's Hospital. They were calling to place an order for 2,500 cookies for an employee appreciation day that was just two days away. I think I laughed at the idea at first, then remembered how much I needed to graduate from my house's outdated desktop to a nice, sleek laptop.

My mom, being the chill lady she is, somehow understood this and agreed we could fill the order. We called our friends Dave and Molly Anderson who owned an amazing, gourmet vegan restaurant called Madeleine Bistro and begged them to borrow their commercial kitchen.

We woke up at 4 a.m., went to Restaurant Depot, loaded up on hundreds of pounds of flour, sugar, and chocolate chips, and went at it. We made chocolate chip cookies and thumbprint cookies. We finished m1aking them at 2 a.m. and delivered them the next m1orning. I bought a MacBook Pro that I use to this day.

Cookies were one of the first sweets I started baking vegan. I remember making some chocolate chip cookies that ended up coming out like scones. My brother ate them. But after a while I figured it out.

I love making cookies because they are the most instantly gratifying dessert out there. You make the cookie dough, eat the cookie dough, bake the cookie dough, and can then eat the fresh baked cookies just a couple of minutes after they get out of the oven. Cookies don't play hard to get.

CHAPTER 1
COOKIES

BROWN BUTTER COOKIES

If you haven't experienced the nutty, warm goodness of brown butter, now is the time. To make brown butter, you cook butter in a saucepan. It adds a rich, caramely flavor to a cookie. I use only brown sugar in this recipe to further enhance the caramel-brown flavor.

1 ¾ cup all-purpose flour
⅔ cup + 2 tablespoons
 v. butter, browned
1 cup dark brown sugar
¼ cup applesauce
1 tablespoon vanilla
 extract
½ teaspoon baking soda
¼ teaspoon salt

Makes 12 large cookies or 24 smallish cookies.

1. Preheat oven to 375 degrees. Line a baking sheet with parchment paper.

2. In a medium saucepan, brown the butter by cooking for 5 to 6 minutes, or until the butter produces a nutty aroma and turns to a deep golden color. This typically happens after the butter's foam bubbles dissolve. Remove from heat and transfer to another bowl immediately, otherwise it'll burn. Stick in fridge.

3. In a medium mixing bowl, whisk together the flour, baking soda, and salt.

4. In large mixing bowl, beat together the brown butter, brown sugar, vanilla extract, and applesauce until completely combined. About 2 minutes.

5. Add the dry ingredients to the wet. Mix together until dough forms.

6. Scoop spoonfuls of cookie dough on the baking sheet about 2 inches apart. Bake for about 6 to 7 minutes, or until edges are nice and brown. Remove from oven and allow to cool on pan for 2 minutes. Transfer to cooling rack.

Despite what you would think, oven temperatures can vary. Some ovens are hotter, some are cooler. While I might say to bake something at a certain temperature, check your baked goods halfway through the baking time to make sure they're not overcooking or undercooking. Adjust temperature accordingly.

COOKIES

These cookies are reminiscent of the outside crispiness and the inner gooeyness of a brownie. They capture all of that, but without having to commit to eating an entire decadent brownie. Unless you stack em and snack em.

BROWNIE COOKIES

1 ½ cup all-purpose flour
½ cup cocoa powder
½ cup brown sugar
½ cup white sugar
⅔ cup v. butter, room
   temperature
¼ cup applesauce
1 tablespoon vanilla
   extract
½ teaspoon baking soda
¼ teaspoon salt
1 cup chocolate chips*

Makes 12 large cookies or 24 smallish cookies.
* Specialty ingredient, buy ahead

1. Preheat oven to 375 degrees. Line a baking sheet with parchment paper.

2. In a medium mixing bowl, whisk together the flour, cocoa powder, baking soda, and salt.

3. Using a stand mixer with paddle attachment, or a rubber spatula and some elbow grease, cream together the butter and sugars until light and fluffy. Make sure to scrape down the sides of the bowl every once in awhile.

4. Add vanilla extract and applesauce to the butter and sugar mixture. Mix on high for about 2 minutes.

5. Slowly add the dry ingredients to the wet and mix until cookie dough forms. Fold in chocolate chips.

6. Scoop spoonfuls of cookie dough onto the baking sheet about 2 inches apart. Bake for about 6-7 minutes, or until edges look done. You may have to lift one up with a spatula to check to see if the bottom of the cookie is cooked.

7. Remove from oven. Let cookies sit on baking pan for two minutes. Transfer to cooling rack.

CHOCOLATE CHIP COOKIES

I'm not sure what it is about fresh chocolate chip cookies that are so addictive, but I can't stop myself from eating them. As soon as I have the cookie dough ready, I'm eating spoonfuls. When they're all warm and fresh out of the oven I grab a stack and go to town and then lay down and try to force myself into a sugar crash induced nap.

These cookies taste like the classic cookie you grew up eating. Or maybe you didn't even grow up eating cookies? I'm sorry! Anyways, they're slightly crunchy on the outside, and chewy and gooey on the inside, and just the right amount of salty. I take my cookies out early so they're extra soft in the middle.

1. Preheat oven to 375 degrees. Line a baking sheet with parchment paper.

2. Using an electric mixer with the whisk attachment, mix together the butter and sugars until smooth and light.

3. Add the applesauce and vanilla extract, mix on high for about a minute. Scrape down sides of the bowl every once in awhile.

4. In a medium mixing bowl, whisk together the flour, baking soda, and salt.

5. Switch the whisk attachment to the paddle attachment or use a rubber spatula and some upper body strength. Add the dry ingredients to the wet, and mix on medium speed until cookie dough comes together. Fold in chocolate chips.

6. Assemble cookie dough by the spoonful and drop 2 inches apart on baking sheet. Bake for about 7 minutes, or until edges are golden brown.

7. Allow to cool on baking pan for 2 minutes. Transfer to cooling rack.

1 ¾ cup all-purpose flour
⅔ cup v. butter, room temperature
¼ cup granulated sugar
¾ cup brown sugar
¼ cup applesauce
1 tablespoon vanilla extract
½ teaspoon baking soda
¼ teaspoon salt
1 cup semi-sweet chocolate chips*

Makes 12 large cookies or 24 smallish cookies.
* Specialty ingredient, buy ahead

INCEPTION COOKIES

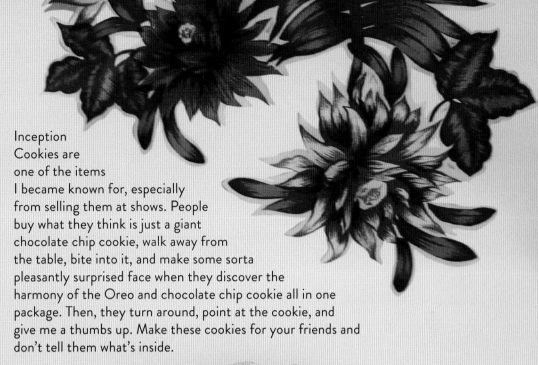

Inception
Cookies are
one of the items
I became known for, especially
from selling them at shows. People
buy what they think is just a giant
chocolate chip cookie, walk away from
the table, bite into it, and make some sorta
pleasantly surprised face when they discover the
harmony of the Oreo and chocolate chip cookie all in one
package. Then, they turn around, point at the cookie, and
give me a thumbs up. Make these cookies for your friends and
don't tell them what's inside.

Make sure to space these cookies out enough. Typically a sheet of cookies fits about 12, but in this case, I'd stick to 9. Otherwise, the cookies' edges will bake together.

2 cup all-purpose flour +
  ½ cup
½ cup brown sugar
½ cup granulated sugar
⅓ cup shortening
⅓ cup v. butter, room
  temperature
¼ cup applesauce
1 tablespoon vanilla
  extract
½ teaspoon baking soda
½ teaspoon salt
1 cup chocolate chips*
15 Oreos

Makes 15 cookies.
* Specialty ingredient, buy
ahead

1. Preheat oven to 350 degrees. Line a baking sheet with parchment paper.

2. Using an electric mixer with the whisk attachment, mix the sugars, shortening, and butter together until light and fluffy. Add in the vanilla extract and applesauce. Mix until fully incorporated.

3. Using a medium mixing bowl, whisk together the 2 cups flour, baking soda, and salt.

4. Switch the whisk attachment to the paddle attachment on the electric mixer or use a rubber spatula and some upper body strength. Add the dry ingredients to the wet ingredients. Mix until the dough is workable, and doesn't stick to your hands. If it does, mix in a handful of flour. Fold in chocolate chips.

5. Place the ½ cup flour in a bowl. Coat your hands with some of the flour.

6. Roll a 2-inch ball of cookie dough, place on one hand, and press lightly using the palm of your other to spread the dough into a circle big enough to fit an Oreo in the center. Wrap the edges of the cookie dough to cover the entire Oreo. It will probably take some extra molding, which is fine. Place cookies 2 inches apart on baking pan. Coat your hands in flour when they get too sticky.

7. Bake for 10 minutes, or until cookies are golden brown. Let sit on pan for 2 minutes, then place cookies on cooling rack.

Italian wedding cookies, also known as Mexican wedding cookies, Russian tea cakes, etc. I don't know who exactly invented the concept of these cookies, but they certainly make me wanna get married so I can feed all this powdery goodness to my homies and get a bunch of powdered sugar all over my wedding dress.

1 cup v. butter
½ cup powdered sugar
  for cookie dough, ½ cup
  for glaze
1 cup finely chopped
  almonds
2 cup all-purpose flour
1 teaspoon vanilla extract

Makes 12–15 medium sized cookies.

1. Preheat oven to 350 degrees. Line a baking sheet with parchment paper.

2. Using an electric mixer with the whisk attachment, mix together powdered sugar and butter until creamy. Add in vanilla extract.

3. One cup at a time, slowly mix the flour and chopped almonds into the butter and powdered sugar mixture. Mix until dough comes together.

4. Shape dough into 2-inch balls. Place about 1 ½ inches apart on baking sheet.

5. Bake for 14-15 minutes, or until the bottoms of the cookies are lightly browned.

6. Let cookies cool on baking sheet for 5 minutes. Roll each cookie in the ½ cup of powdered sugar until evenly coated. Place on cooling rack.

COOKIES

ITALIAN WEDDING COOKIES

PIGNOLI COOKIES

While I'm only a quarter Italian, I really hold onto that fact tightly because of the beauty of Italian cuisine. I wasn't raised eating "authentic" Italian food by any means. I'm probably mostly made of boxed pasta and jarred marinara sauce.

I gotta be honest, I did try to attempt to do a vegan version of the classic egg white-almond paste-sugar pignoli cookie, but I realized halfway through it how much I dislike the taste of almonds in the form of extract or paste. It's got this cherry-like taste to it that I don't find tasty. This is my take on a pignoli cookie. It has white cornmeal in it that gives it an extra crunch and works with the pine nuts really well. It's like a fancy version of sugar cookies.

1 cup all-purpose flour
¼ cup pine nuts + 1 cup for rolling
¼ cup white cornmeal
1 tablespoon flaxseed meal + 3 tablespoon warm water
½ cup sugar
½ cup v. butter
½ teaspoon baking soda
zest of half a lemon
pinch of nutmeg

Makes 12 large cookies or 24 smallish cookies.

1. Preheat oven to 350 degrees. Line a baking sheet with parchment paper.

2. Mix together the flaxseed meal and warm water. Let sit for five minutes.

3. In a food processor, pulse the ¼ cup pine nuts, flour, cornmeal, baking soda, and nutmeg together until pine nuts are just about ground.

4. Using an electric mixer, cream together the sugar and butter on medium speed until creamy. Add in the flax seed mix until light and fluffy. Add in the lemon zest and mix until incorporated.

5. Add the dry ingredients to the wet. Mix until dough comes together.

6. Roll cookie dough into 2-inch balls. Lightly roll dough in pine nuts. Place on baking sheet about 2 inches apart.

7. Bake for about 7-10 minutes, or until edges are golden brown. Allow to cool on baking sheet for 2 minutes. Transfer to cooling rack.

WHITE CHOC
CRA

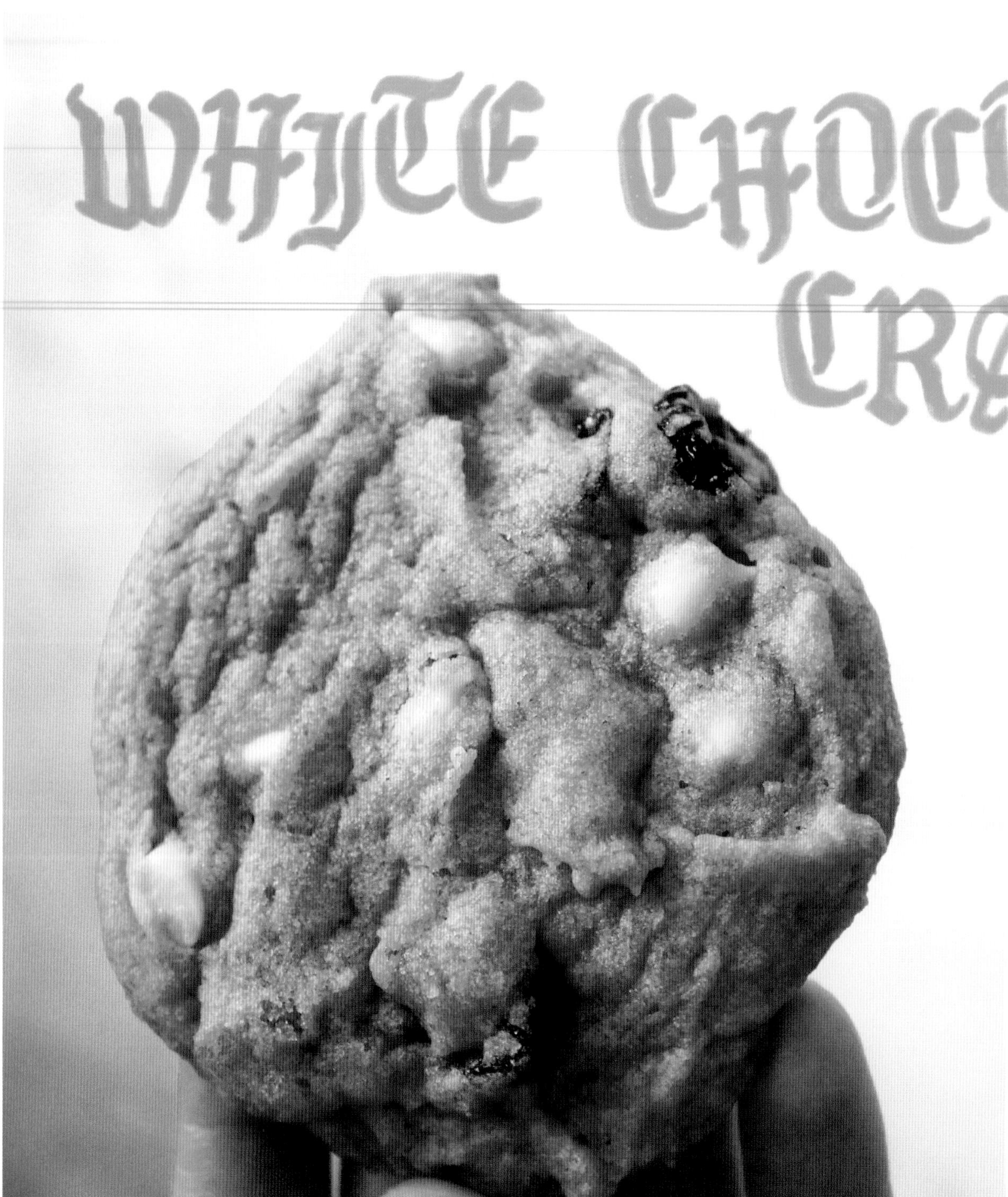

LATE NBERRY COOKIES

I imagine these cookies enclosed in a circular tin box with a bow wrapped around for a Christmas gift. If you truly know me, you know that I don't like raisins. For whatever reason, craisins make the cut. They have a tanginess to them that plain ol' raisins lack. You can either use freeze-dried cranberries for these cookies which are nice and crunchy, or craisins. Christmas in a cookie!

1. Preheat oven to 375 degrees. Line a baking sheet with parchment paper.

2. In a medium mixing bowl, whisk together the flour, baking soda, and salt.

3. Using an electric mixer, cream together the butter, sugars, applesauce, and vanilla extract on medium speed until well incorporated.

4. Add the dry ingredients to the wet and mix until just combined. Fold in the craisins and white chocolate chips.

5. Scoop spoonfuls of the dough onto the baking sheet, about 2 inches apart. Bake for 7-10 minutes, or until edges are golden brown.

6. Allow cookies to cool on pan for 2 minutes. Then transfer to a cooling rack.

1 ¾ cup all-purpose flour
½ cup granulated sugar
½ cup brown sugar
¼ cup applesauce
⅔ cup v. butter, room temperature
1 cup white chocolate chips*
1 tablespoon vanilla extract
½ teaspoon baking soda
½ teaspoon salt

Makes 12 large cookies or 24 smallish cookies.
* Specialty ingredient, buy ahead

WHY I'M VEGAN

The longer I'm vegan, the more I'm worried about coming off as "preachy." Whether I'm catering a music fest or selling sweets at a pop-up, I don't advertise anything I'm serving as vegan. Most vegan people will ask if I have anything they can eat, and then they find they can eat everything!

But the bottom line is I wouldn't be doing what I'm doing if it weren't for becoming vegan. While there are all sorts of great benefits, I didn't become vegan for health or clearer skin.

Since explaining myself might help you to get to know me and better understand my baking, here it goes.

I became vegan because:

Cows do not naturally produce milk regularly. I was completely surprised when I found out dairy cows have to birth a calf in order to produce breast milk, which is the milk we drink. The calf is taken away within hours of its birth, leaving the mother cow in mourning often leading to depression. If the calf is male, it will live its very short life in a crate before becoming veal. If it's a female, it will live the same life as its mother. A dairy cow's life span is about five years, compared to a life expectancy of roughly twenty years under natural conditions. The dairy industry literally milks the cow for all it is worth during this time. Those five years are a relentless cycle of impregnation, birth, and milking. When the mama cow can no longer carry a pregnancy, she is sent to slaughter.

The cow's process of creating breast milk is no different than the one our mothers had. The milk they produce is meant to be consumed by their baby, not a human.

The egg industry. A century ago, hens laid around 100 eggs every year. At present, due to breeding and hormone therapy, they lay closer to 250. Most egg-laying hens live their entire lives in tiny, crowded wire cages with five to ten other hens. They have no way to escape painful feather loss, bruises, and abrasions, before they are ultimately slaughtered.

The environment. It takes over 2,400 gallons of water to produce one pound of meat. Additionally, factory farm animals produce one million tons of manure per day, creating harmful greenhouse gases and unsecured collection pools of toxic waste.

Employee mistreatment. Employees at factory farms work ten hour-plus days, often making around just $23,000 per year, and oftentimes without so much as a bathroom break.

We have built an agricultural system that is completely dependent on *numbers*, speeding up life cycles while squeezing everything we can out of these animals. In the midst of this, we have forgotten that each one of these "numbers" feels pain and grief, and is a living, breathing being.

By controlling my diet, I'm able to withdraw my support from unnecessary suffering, unfair labor, and a negative environmental impact. What I've learned from being vegan eight years is that it's not a sacrifice by any means. I've eaten the best food, cooked the best meals, and have felt the healthiest in this time, and there were no animals harmed in any part of that.

BARS

CHAPTER 2

Bars are always one of the first things I sell out of when I bring them to an event. They're very portable and very delicious. You can take a crazy cookie idea, throw it into a pan, and call it a bar. They're practically cookie casseroles!

So many of these bar recipes were made based on me going to a cafe, looking at their un-vegan pastry case, and wanting them so much that I'd go home and make them my way.

BARS

BROWN BUTTER PUMPKIN PIE BAR

These pumpkin pie bars are very similar to a classic pumpkin pie, except the crust is a brown sugar brown butter shortbread crust. While you get a nice melt-in-your-mouth crumble from the crust, you also get extra warmth from the addition of brown butter. And I sneak some vegan cream cheese into the filling. It carries all the flavors of the pumpkin and spices through, like a nice, big hug. Much love to a handheld, square, pie treat.

Brown butter is what you get when you cook butter on the stove for about five minutes. It melts, starts to foam, and eventually breaks down and release a nutty aroma.

Crust:
1 ¼ cup all-purpose flour
⅓ cup dark brown sugar
10 tablespoon v. butter, browned
¼ teaspoon salt

Filling:
1 cup + 3 tablespoons canned pumpkin
½ cup brown sugar
¼ cup v. cream cheese*
3 tablespoon coconut cream
1 tablespoon v. butter, room temperature
1 ½ tablespoons cornstarch
½ tablespoon vanilla extract
1 ½ teaspoon cinnamon
¼ teaspoon ground ginger
¼ teaspoon nutmeg
pinch of ground cloves
pinch of salt

Toppings:
½ cup pecans, chopped
2 tablespoon dark brown sugar
2 tablespoon v. butter, browned

Specialty ingredient, buy ahead

CRUST

1. Preheat oven to 350 degrees. Spray an 8x8 baking pan with nonstick spray. Line with a parchment paper square.

2. In a medium saucepan, brown the butter by cooking for 5 to 6 minutes, or until the butter produces a nutty aroma and turns to a deep golden color. This typically happens after the butter's foam bubbles dissolve. Remove from heat and transfer to another bowl immediately, otherwise it'll burn. Stick in fridge.

3. In a large bowl, combine the flour, brown sugar, and salt. Add in the brown butter and stir until the mixture can be pinched together. Press mixture firmly into bottom of the pan. Bake for about 20 minutes. Remove and let cool.

FILLING

4. While the crust is baking, prepare filling. Using an electric mixer with the whisk attachment, mix together all filling ingredients on high. The cream cheese will take some time to completely blend, but it's well worth it.

5. Pour filling onto baked crust. Place in oven for about 35-45 minutes, or until filling is set.

TOPPING

6. While the bars are baking, prepare the topping. In a small bowl, toss the pecans in the brown sugar and butter until fully coated.

7. Remove bars from oven, sprinkle with pecan topping, and bake for about 5 more minutes.

8. Remove pan from oven and allow to cool on rack for one hour. Store in refrigerator.

I never fail to burn the roof of my mouth because I just can't wait five minutes to try a bite of hot, fresh, gooey brownies. There's something special about the brownie eating experience. It's like your taste buds wrap themselves tightly around the brownie as soon as you take a bite and you don't really have to chew it much, so it gives you longer to savor the decadence.

These brownies are cake brownies. I know some people get kinda serious about fudge brownies vs. cake brownies but I love them all. It's 2017: time to accept all brownies!

BARS

Bake for 25-30 minutes. It's super easy to overcook brownies because it's hard to tell if they're gooey or not. They're done baking when the top of the brownies is a little cracked, and the middle is set.

BROWNIES

Preheat oven to 350 degrees. Coat a 9x9 baking pan with nonstick spray. Lay a parchment paper square over the pan to prevent brownies from sticking.

1. In a small bowl mix together the flax meal and applesauce. Set aside.

2. Stir the flour, cocoa powder, sugar, baking soda, baking powder, and salt together in a medium bowl.

3. In a separate medium bowl, whisk together the flax-applesauce mixture, soymilk, coconut milk, butter, and vanilla extract.

4. Add the wet mixture to the dry. Stir until just combined.

5. Pour brownie batter into pan. Bake for 25 minutes. Don't burn your mouth.

1 ¼ cup all-purpose flour
1 cup sugar
½ cup cocoa powder
½ cup soymilk
½ cup + 2 tablespoon v. butter, melted
¼ cup canned coconut milk
¼ cup applesauce
2 tablespoon ground flax meal
1 tablespoon vanilla extract
1 teaspoon baking soda
1 teaspoon salt
¼ teaspoon baking powder

POTATO CHIP BLONDIES

It's kinda crazy to me how a lot of people have never heard of "blondies" before. In case you're one of those people, it's basically a chocolate chip cookie bar, except, sometimes the chocolate is replaced by nuts, or, sometimes it has both. In this case, it has potato chips and chocolate chips.

In preschool, there were the kids that dipped their pretzels in apple juice, and then the ones that didn't. I was one of the pretzel-apple juice kids. I've loved the combo of sweet and salty as long as I can remember. This bar is like a perfect, extra thick, chocolate chip cookie with the consistency of a brownie, and an extra crispiness and saltiness from the potato chip to even it all out. Bonus points: dip in apple juice. I'm kidding! Don't do that! Dip in soymilk!

1. Preheat your oven to 350 degrees. Line a 9x9 pan with a coat of nonstick spray, then line with a parchment paper square.

2. In a small bowl mix together the egg replacer powder and the hot water for about a minute or so. You want the mixture to be smooth and slightly thick. The key is to mix enough so that the powder is fully blended, otherwise you'll end up with clumps of powder in the batter.

¼ cup egg replacer
¼ cup hot water
½ cup v. butter, melted
  with ½ cup brown sugar
⅓ cup white sugar
1 tablespoon vanilla
  extract
1 cup all-purpose flour
½ teaspoon baking soda
½ teaspoon salt
1 cup semi-sweet
  chocolate chips*
1 cup (or 3 handfuls)
  Ruffles (or any potato
  chip with ridges)

*Specialty ingredient, buy
ahead*

3. In a mixing bowl combine the melted butter/brown sugar mixture with the white sugar. Mix until combined. Add the vanilla extract and the egg replacer mixture and stir until combined.

4. In a separate bowl sift together the flour, baking soda, and salt (sifting is when you put dry ingredients through a special strainer that makes flour and such smaller, which gives you a lighter end result).

5. Add the dry ingredients to the wet and mix until *just* combined. Now add in the chocolate chips. Add in the potato chips, crushing them up with your hands.

6. Spread the batter in the pan with a spatula, making it nice and even on top. Bake for about 30-35 minutes. It should look golden brown on top, like how you would like a batch of cookies to look. Once done, place the pan on a cooling rack.

BARS

As a kid, my gingerbread houses were always the sloppiest. I'd go into decorating mode with solid ideas, and somewhere in the mess of the glaze and candy I'd lose momentum. It's kinda the way everything goes for me, especially decoration wise.

Ginger blondies are if a gingerbread man got with a blondie (the cookie bar, of course!) and had a beautiful, chubby baby. I love this baby because it's not as crunchy as a gingerbread cookie. Instead, it's rich and gooey and the ginger spice will have your taste buds ticklish. These make for perfect Christmas and winter treats!

2 ¾ cup all-purpose flour

1 ¼ teaspoon baking soda

1 ¼ teaspoon salt

2 teaspoon ground cinnamon

1 teaspoon ground ginger

½ teaspoon ground cloves

1 ½ cup v. butter, room temperature

1 cup dark brown sugar

1 cup molasses

¼ cup granulated sugar

1 ½ teaspoon Ener-G egg replacer* + 2 tablespoon warm water

1 tablespoon flaxseed, mixed with 3 tablespoon warm water

½ tablespoon pure vanilla extract

Glaze:

½ cup powdered sugar

2 tablespoon soymilk

⅛ teaspoon vanilla extract

Specialty ingredient, buy ahead

1. Preheat oven to 350 degrees. Spray a 13x9 baking pan with nonstick spray and a parchment paper rectangle.

2. Prepare the flaxseed and water by stirring together with a fork in a small bowl. In another bowl, do the same for the Ener-G egg replacer.

3. In a medium bowl, whisk together the flour, baking soda, salt, cinnamon, ginger, and cloves.

4. Using an electric mixer with the whisk attachment, beat the butter, sugars, and molasses together on medium speed until light and fluffy.

5. Add vanilla to the butter, then add in the egg replacer. Beat until fully incorporated, about 2 minutes.

6. Slowly mix the dry ingredients into the wet. Beat on low speed until fully combined.

7. Spread batter into pan. Bake for about 25 minutes. Place on cooling rack when out of oven.

8. While the ginger blondies are cooling, make the glaze. Stir together the powdered sugar, soymilk, and vanilla until smooth.

9. Drizzle glaze over bars when they're fully cooled. Slice and serve.

BARS

GINGER BLONDIES

Molasses is messy!

I rarely ate traditional s'mores growing up because:

1. Marshmallows have gelatin, and

2. I've never been camping in my life.

What I can remember of these sweet snacks is that the marshmallow always swallowed up all the other flavors. It was too sweet to be able to enjoy the perfect graham cracker and melty chocolate combo. These s'mores bars give you a balanced ratio of a lot of graham-cookie-bar crust, just enough chocolate chips, and a bit of melty marshmallow to tuck it in. I honestly don't have much of a desire to ever go camping since I can just make these bars in my oven...

1 cup crushed Nabisco plain graham cracker crumbs
1 cup all-purpose flour
1 cup semi-sweet chocolate chips*
1 cup Dandies Marshmallows,* torn in half
1 cup brown sugar
½ cup v. butter, melted
1 tablespoon coconut vinegar
1 teaspoon baking soda
1 teaspoon baking powder

Specialty ingredient, buy ahead

1. Preheat oven to 350 degrees. Spray a 9x9 baking pan with nonstick spray and line with parchment paper.

2. In a small bowl, stir together the vinegar and baking soda with a fork. The baking soda will dissolve. Set aside.

3. In a medium bowl, stir together the graham cracker crumbs, flour, and baking powder.

4. Using an electric mixer, cream together the butter and sugar on medium speed until light and fluffy.

5. Add the vinegar and baking soda mixture to the butter and beat on high until the vinegar is fully incorporated, about two minutes.

6. Slowly add in the dry ingredients on medium speed and beat until it looks like cookie dough.

7. Reserve ¼ of the dough and set aside, you'll use this later for the topping. Press the remaining dough into the baking pan.

8. Sprinkle chocolate chips and marshmallows evenly onto the cookie dough layer.

9. Take the cookie dough you set aside and scatter grape-sized pieces over the marshmallows and chocolate chips.

10. Bake for 25 minutes or until golden brown. Place on cooling rack, serve warm.

BARS

If you can't find Nabisco plain graham crackers, you can sub Golden Grahams. I think they pack even more flavor in! You'll want to purchase Dandies Marshmallows from a health food store or online ahead of time.

S'MORES BAR

BARS

SPICED DATE BAR

Dates were one of those things I was afraid to try for a really long time. It was on the same list as avocado. When I finally tried them, I was hooked. They're like little, natural caramels.

On our way home from a mini trip to Joshua Tree, my mom and I stopped at Hadley's Fruit Orchards Market. I was in date heaven. I grabbed some date paste and made date bars as soon as we got home. I ate half a pan in one day and wish I was joking!

Date filling:
1 ½ cup date paste
½ cup warm water
1 tablespoon lemon juice
½ teaspoon cinnamon
¼ teaspoon nutmeg
¼ teaspoon ginger
¼ teaspoon allspice
pinch of cloves
pinch of salt

Crust:
1 ¾ cup whole wheat flour
1 ½ cup oatmeal
1 cup v. butter
1 cup dark brown sugar
1 teaspoon vanilla extract
½ teaspoon baking soda
½ teaspoon salt
½ teaspoon cinnamon

1. Preheat oven to 400 degrees. Spray a 13x9 baking pan with nonstick spray. Line pan with parchment paper.

2. Combine the date paste, water, lemon, spices, and salt in a medium mixing bowl. Mix until the paste is spreadable and easy to work with.

3. In a large mixing bowl, whisk together the flour, oatmeal, baking soda, salt, and cinnamon. Set aside.

4. Using an electric mixer, cream together the brown sugar and butter until creamy.

5. Add the dry ingredients to the butter and sugar. Mix until the crust stays together when pinched.

6. Set ¼ of the crust aside. Press the remainder of the dough in the baking pan evenly. Spread the date paste filling on top. Sprinkle the remainder of the crust on top of the date paste layer.

7. Bake for 25-30 minutes or until golden brown. Place on cooling rack.

STRAWBERRY BLOOD ORANGE BAR

These bars were born out of my love for seasonal fruits. When coming up with my Valentine's Day menu, I always check and see what fruits and citruses are in season. February is the month of strawberries and blood oranges. So darn sexy!

I can totally remember making these bars for the first time. I was thinking about what crust would compliment such a beautiful fruit filling, and ideas kept pouring out. It resulted in a delicious white cornmeal, oatmeal, and flour crust that's held together by a combination of coconut oil and butter. The hint of coconut and the crunch of the cornmeal compliment the strawberry and blood orange filling perfectly. A match made in heaven!

Be ready to eat this on a plate with a fork. While they're bars, the nature of the delicious cornmeal crust makes them a bit more messy and crumbly than most. Bonus points if you serve these with vanilla ice cream! Make these in February! It's blood orange season then and also Valentine's Day!

1 cup all-purpose flour +
  3 tablespoons flour
1 ½ cup oatmeal
½ cup white cornmeal
1 cup brown sugar
1 teaspoon baking
  powder
½ teaspoon salt
½ cup v. butter, chopped
  into small cubes
⅓ cup coconut oil
¾ cup strawberry
  preserves
½ cup fresh strawberries,
  chopped
3 blood oranges, peeled
  and chopped

1. Preheat oven to 350 degrees. Spray a 13x9 baking pan with nonstick spray. Line pan with parchment paper.

2. In a large bowl, mix together 1 cup flour with the oatmeal, cornmeal, brown sugar, baking powder, and salt.

3. Mix in the coconut oil and butter, pressing the mixture together with your fingers. Mix until it resembles crumbly cookie dough. If mixture is too dry to be pinched together, add a tad more butter or coconut oil.

4. Press half of the oat mixture into pan. Set aside.

5. In a medium bowl, stir together the strawberry jam, fresh strawberries, oranges, and 3 tablespoons flour until evenly incorporated.

6. Spread the preserves mixture over the oat crust. Sprinkle the other half of the oat mixture on top.

7. Bake until golden brown, about 30-40 minutes. Place on cooling rack and serve warm or fully cooled.

BARS

BAKING MIX

I credit my brother Andy for influencing my music taste. Driving in his car is always fun because I get to ask him typical little sister questions like, "Who is this?" which he'll most likely reply to with the artist's name, album, and year it came out. And don't get him started on Neil Young!

Since my brother is one of the most musically knowledgeable people I know, I had him making a baking mix. His DJ name is DJ Drew Time. Love you bro!

"Jet Ski" — Bikini Kill
"The Third" — Silkworm
"Girlfriend" — Eric's Trip
"Star Fed" — Sustains
"Cities in Dust" — Siouxsie and the Banshees
"Legends of My Own" — Gun Outfit
"Preservation" — The Kinks
"Dark End of the Street" — The Flying Burrito Brothers
"The Glory of Man" — Minutemen
"Frontwards" — Pavement
"6 O'Clock News" — Red C
"No Side to Fall In" — The Raincoats
"So You Say You Lost Your Baby" — Gene Clark
"Tragic Carpet Ride" — Polvo
"Baud to Tears" — The Verlaines
"Follow the Locust" — Wire

claracakes.com

CHAPTER 3

It's hard to eat cakes without a pudding or fruit sauce sandwiched in. They carry you from the cake into the frosting. To me, cakes feel incomplete without it.

You can get pretty spontaneous with the fruit sauce recipes in here, according to what's in season where you live. It's fun making the most of whatever delicious fruits are available by cooking them into a sauce. I love when a vanilla cake perfectly soaks up a fresh fruit filling.

Pudding, on the other hand, is pudding. Why wouldn't you want a chocolate layer in a vanilla cake?

If you plan on refrigerating pudding and fruit sauce for over an hour, it will thicken even more. If this happens, I suggest stirring a little soymilk into pudding before serving to ensure it's nice and creamy. For fruit sauces, add a tad bit of water.

PUDDINGS

AND SAUCES

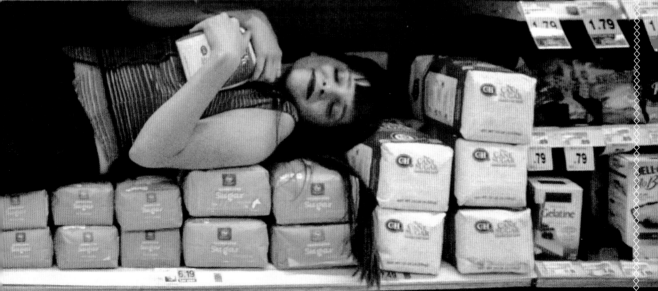

Chocolate pudding is like a brownie batter smoothie, blended to a creamy perfection. Sometimes I have leftover chocolate pudding in the fridge from a batch on Neapolitan cupcakes (pg. 132) and it truly makes my entire day.

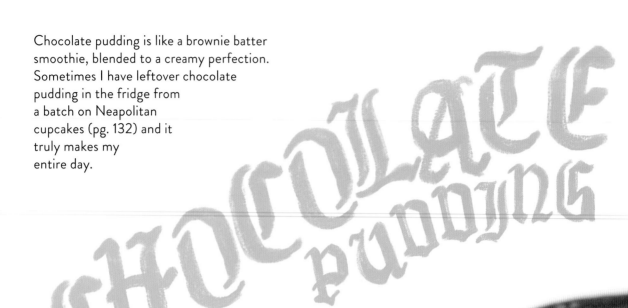

CHOCOLATE PUDDING

⅓ cup cocoa powder
⅓ cup sugar
¾ cup coconut milk
¾ cup soymilk
2 tablespoon + 2
  teaspoon cornstarch
⅛ teaspoon salt
1 teaspoon v. butter

Makes 2 cups of sauce.

1. In a medium saucepan, whisk together the cocoa powder, sugar, salt, and cornstarch.

2. On medium heat, whisk in the milks and stir constantly until thickened to pudding consistency.

3. Remove from heat and whisk in vanilla extract and butter.

4. Place a sheet of plastic wrap directly on surface of pudding to prevent a skin from forming. Refrigerate until ready to serve.

HORCHATA PUDDING

Make Horchata in advance!

This pudding is so delicious that you don't even have to pair it with cake, necessarily. However, it creates the ultimate blanket of cinnamon custard goodness in between two horchata cake (pg. 128) layers.

1. In a medium saucepan stir the sugar, cornstarch, and salt together. Whisk in the horchata over medium heat, stirring constantly until mixture is thick and pudding-like.

2. Remove from heat and stir in butter and vanilla.

3. Transfer pudding to a bowl and cover with plastic wrap directly on the surface of the pudding. Store in refrigerator.

1 ½ cup horchata (see below)
⅓ cup sugar
2 tablespoon + 2 teaspoon cornstarch
1 teaspoon v. butter
1 teaspoon vanilla
⅛ teaspoon salt

Makes 2 cups of sauce.

HORCHATA

1. Mix together the rice and water in a big bowl. Cover and let soak overnight.

2. Blend the water and rice on high for about 3 minutes. The rice should be really blended. The grain won't go away completely, but for the most part it should be gone.

3. Pour into a large bowl and mix in the soymilk and sugar until completely combined. Keep refrigerated.

Horchata:
1 cup white rice
2 cup water
4 teaspoon cinnamon
¼ cup sugar
2 cup soymilk

STRAW BERRY SAUCE

This recipe doesn't specifically go on any of the more complex cakes. But I feel like strawberry sauce is a cake-making skill essential. You can make a strawberry shortcake style cake with it, top it on countless other frosting flavors, even drizzle it on some ice cream!

While I understand the convenience of frozen strawberries, this recipe uses fresh strawberries for a reason. The fresh, crushed strawberries are able to thicken in their own bloody, sweet, sauce with the help of some strawberry preserves and a tiny bit of sugar.

1. In a saucepan, stir together the strawberries, preserves, water, and sugar.

2. Cook on medium heat, stirring occasionally.

3. The mixture will start to thicken at the 7-minute mark. Start stirring constantly then.

4. Remove from heat. Store in airtight container or serve right away.

1 cup fresh crushed strawberries
¼ cup strawberry preserves
1 tablespoon sugar
2 tablespoon water

Makes 1 cup of sauce.

SEXY SAUCE

When I was planning what to bring to my first Los Angeles Vegan Beer & Food Festival, I had a couple guidelines. I needed to make desserts that would appeal to people drinking, when they really crave things like fries and pretzels. My answer to that was the sexy cake (pg. 142). It's a key lime cake, filled with sexy sauce: blueberries, key lime juice and zest, sugar, salt, and cayenne pepper, and topped with key lime frosting and more sexy sauce swirled in. It's salty, tangy, spicy, and sweet all in one bite. Goes perfect with a cold beer.

1. In a medium saucepan, gently combine the blueberries, sugar, key lime juice, cayenne pepper, salt, and lime zest. Allow to simmer for an hour on medium to low heat, stirring every now and then.

2. When mixture has thickened, remove from heat and store in refrigerator.

1 container fresh blueberries
¼ cup sugar
½ cup key lime juice
¼ teaspoon cayenne pepper
½ teaspoon salt
zest of 1 key lime

Makes 1 cup of sauce.

You can use this recipe for practically anything breakfast related. Toss some cereal on top, put it on some pancakes, even sandwich it between a couple waffles. I use it for the breakfast cake (pg. 122).

⅓ cup brown sugar
¾ cup soymilk
¾ cup canned coconut milk
2 tablespoon + 2 teaspoon cornstarch
⅛ teaspoon salt
1 teaspoon v. butter
1 teaspoon vanilla extract
1 ½ teaspoon maple extract

Makes 2 cups of sauce.

1. In a medium saucepan, whisk together the sugar, cornstarch, and salt.

2. Whisk in the coconut milk and soymilk over medium heat.

3. Stir constantly until the mixture is thick and pudding-like. Turn off heat and whisk in vanilla extract, maple extract, and butter until combined.

4. Transfer to a bowl and put plastic wrap directly on the entire surface of pudding. This prevents pudding skin from forming. Store in refrigerator.

MAPLE MILK PUDDING

PUDDINGS AND SAUCES

VANILLA PUDDING

I've always been a big pudding fan. Before I was vegan, I'd eat Snack Pack puddings in probably two big spoonfuls. Best school snack dessert to top off a bag of chips.

I use this recipe for cake fillings, pie custards, and my belly for an easy sweet snack.

⅓ cup sugar
2 tablespoon + 2 teaspoon cornstarch
¾ cup soymilk
¾ cup canned coconut milk
1 teaspoon vanilla extract
1 teaspoon v. butter
⅛ teaspoon salt

Makes 2 cups of sauce.

1. In a medium saucepan, whisk together the sugar, salt, and cornstarch.

2. On medium heat, whisk in the soymilk and coconut milk.

3. Stir constantly until the mixture thickens into pudding, about 5 minutes. Remove from heat and whisk in the vanilla extract and butter.

4. Cover with plastic wrap directly on the surface of the pudding to prevent a skin from forming. Refrigerate until serving.

DIY MUSIC = DIY BAKING

I've grown up in very punk households. My mom was a part-time new waver, part-time punker. She even met Nirvana—before they blew up. My dad is a drummer and was in a couple bands, and jams to this day. Both of my brothers are musicians, with their talents spanning from guitar to bass to drums to vocals. I still enjoy blasting pop music here and there to spice it up some, but the punk ethos was instilled in me from a young age, whether I liked it or not.

But it wasn't until I was about 12 years old that I really began to learn about and appreciate the way different musicians and labels—not just punks—ran their businesses to keep tours and recording afloat.

When I first started thinking about baking I was really thinking about the 1990s riot grrrl movement. The riot grrrl philosophy was that my voice and vision should be shared with the world, and self-publishing art, writing, and even recipes was important even if no one read them.

When I realized baking was becoming more than a hobby and could become a business, I was most influenced by the DIY ethos of the punk band Minutemen, who had a strong econo work ethic. I related to their working-class roots, and admired that they still worked day jobs when not touring. Their idea of making a record so that they could promote a tour inspired me to do some baking so that I could make the trip to LA and sell at one of my favorite bands' shows. I hand-printed and hand-cut some janky business cards in the beginning, gave them out, and even funded a school trip to NYC through a bake sale I hosted.

When you grow up working-class, there's really no other way than the DIY way. I think the beauty of it for so many bands, creatives, and businesses is that you don't even realize you're following a certain ethos, you're just thinking practically and resourcefully. And in the end, I think all that personal hard work makes it feel even more special to you and the people that helped you.

Back when I was a little kid, my Dad would go nuts over the Marie Callender's pie sale. There would always be two specific pies we'd get: chocolate cream pie and banana cream pie. My dad would store the pies in our sticker-covered garage fridge.

I'd go in the kitchen, grab a fork, and quietly walk to the door leading to the garage—making sure to close it behind me quietly. As I opened the fridge, there lay the holy grail: the two Marie Callender's bakery boxes with the logo and a drawing of some fruit on them. I'd open each box just enough to get my fork inside and carve out a bite, scraping some excess whipped cream off on the way. I'd take my delicately balanced fork and eat my bite atop a big tire attached to the skeleton of the old Chevy truck my dad was fixing up.

Ever since then, cream pies have seemed like a very special, almost forbidden dessert to me. The light whipped cream, and the cold, smooth pudding, on top of a perfectly flaky, butter crust brings me back to those adventures I'd have in the garage.

CHAPTER 4
PIES

Back when I was experimenting for one of my pop-up brunches, I thought of a really yummy pie crust idea: Cap'n Crunch crust. Originally I paired it with the banana cream filling, which was super delicious, but then I thought "What if I pulse Cap'n Crunch, butter, aaaand peanut butter together?" So I tried it and the flavor was surprisingly familiar. It tasted just like the crispy, peanut butter cookie in Butterfingers. From there, this recipe was a no-brainer—Butterfinger pie it is.

Crust:
6 cup Cap'n Crunch
  cereal
¼ cup smooth peanut
  butter
½ cup melted v. butter

Filling:
8 ounce v. cream cheese*
½ cup smooth peanut
  butter
9 ounce v. whipped
  cream*
¾ cup powdered sugar
1 teaspoon vanilla extract
1 tablespoon soymilk

Sauce:
½ cup chocolate chips*
¼ cup soymilk
1 tablespoon v. butter

*Specialty ingredient
  buy ahead

CRUST

1. Preheat oven to 350 degrees.

2. In a food processor, pulse the Cap'n Crunch until it's mostly crumbs.

3. Add the peanut butter and butter and pulse for about 3 minutes. The mixture should just about stick together. Set aside about ½ cup of the mixture for the topping later on.

4. Press the pie crust into a pie tin and bake for about 3-5 minutes. When the crust looks like it's cooked together nicely, and is slightly browned, it's ready. Place on cooling rack.

FILLING

1. In an electric mixer using the whisk attachment, cream together the peanut butter and cream cheese. Blend until smooth.

2. Add the whipped cream, soymilk, vanilla extract, and powdered sugar. Mix until completely smooth, light, and fluffy.

SAUCE

1. Cook soymilk in small saucepan until it just starts to boil. Remove from heat and stir in chocolate chips until they're completely melted. Mix in the butter. Set aside.

2. Pour the peanut butter filling into the crust. Spread evenly. Drizzle chocolate sauce over. Sprinkle the Butterfinger crust mixture on top. Chill in fridge for a few hours or overnight before serving.

BUTTERFINGER PIE

CHOCOLATE CREAM PIE

I really love chocolate cream pie as an alternative to chocolate cake. It's just as decadent, but feels a bit lighter. The perfectly sweet and chocolatey pudding is brought out even more with the flaky, slightly salty, delicate crust.

CRUST

1. In a medium bowl, whisk together the flour, sugar, and salt.

2. Add in the cold butter cubes. Incorporate butter into flour my using your fingers, or by pulsing a few times in a food processor. Mix until it becomes course meal.

3. Add in ice water 1 tablespoon at a time. Stop adding water when the dough comes together. You want to steer clear of wet dough and dough that easily falls apart. You want a happy medium to achieve a flaky crust.

4. Knead the dough once or twice, then shape into a ball and wrap in plastic wrap. Store in the fridge for 2 days or overnight.

5. Preheat oven to 375. Get your pie tin out.

6. Using a rolling pin roll the dough out on a flat surface lightly coated in flour. Roll into the best circle you can make. Gently pick up the dough and place on the pie tin. Press and pinch til pretty and smooth.

7. Put a sheet of aluminum paper over the pie dough, and then spread pie weights over the foil. This will prevent the dough from bubbling up. Cook the dough for 16-20 minutes, or until the edges are nice and golden. Remove from oven and place on cooling rack.

FILLING

1. In a medium saucepan, stir the cocoa powder, cornstarch, sugar, and salt together. Whisk in the coconut milk and soymilk. Stir constantly for about five minutes. Turn off heat when the mixture is a really thick, pudding paste.

2. In a food processor, blend the tofu and the chocolate pudding paste together until very smooth. Add in the maple syrup, melted butter, and vanilla extract. Blend til smooth, making sure to scrape the sides of the bowl down. Taste and adjust sugar and salt accordingly.

3. Pour the chocolate pudding mixture into the pie crust. Refrigerate overnight.

Top pie with whipped cream and chocolate shavings before serving.

Crust:
1 ¼ cup all-purpose flour
½ teaspoon sugar
¼ teaspoon salt
3-4 tablespoon ice-cold water
½ cup v. butter, chopped into cubes and froze for 5 minutes

Filling:
1 cup canned coconut milk
½ cup soymilk + ½ cup soymilk
1 cup sugar
⅓ cup cocoa powder
¼ teaspoon salt
½ cup + 3 tablespoon cornstarch
1 package Mori-Nu Extra Firm Silken Tofu*
½ cup maple syrup
2 tablespoon v. butter, melted
1 ½ tablespoon vanilla extract

Topping:
v. whipped cream*
dark chocolate

*Specialty ingredient buy ahead

CHOCOLATE RICOTTA CHEESECAKE

Vegan ricotta cheese:
1 cup raw, whole soaked
 cashews
½ cup raw, soaked
 slivered almonds
½ cup water
juice of ½ lemon
1 teaspoon salt

Crust:
1 ½ cup all-purpose flour
¾ cup pine nuts, normal
¾ cup pine nuts, toasted
2 tablespoon white
 cornmeal
¼ cup brown sugar
⅔ cup v. butter, melted

Filling:
v. ricotta cheese (see
 above)
6 ounce Mori-Nu Extra
 Firm Silken Tofu*
8 ounce v. cream cheese*
2 teaspoon agar-agar
 powder*
1 cup sugar
¼ cup water
1 teaspoon salt
1 ¼ cup semi-sweet
 chocolate chips*

*Specialty ingredient
 buy ahead*

This recipe means a lot to me. I came up with it while building my menu for my pop-up dinner in Las Vegas at the amazing restaurant VegeNation. It was the first time I was able to present my Italian cooking in a restaurant environment, and this cheesecake topped it all off.

VEGAN RICOTTA CHEESE

1. In a food processor, pulse the cashews and almonds together. Keep pulsing until they become less gritty and more creamy.

2. Slowly add in water and pulse. Keep pulsing until the mixture has a ricotta-like texture.

3. Pulse in the lemon juice and salt, taste test, and adjust accordingly. Transfer to bowl and refrigerate.

CRUST

1. Preheat oven to 350 degrees.

2. In a food processor, pulse the pine nuts, cornmeal, flour, and sugar together until incorporated. Pulse in the butter until you can pinch the mixture together without it falling apart.

3. Press into a pie or tart pan. Cover with aluminum foil and pie weights and bake for 25 minutes or until golden.

4. Allow crust to cool on cooling rack and prepare the cheesecake filling in the meantime.

Make sure to soak your cashews and almonds ahead of time to activate. 8 hours-overnight is best.

Filling

1. In a small saucepan, stir together the sugar and water on medium heat until sugar is completely dissolved. Set aside.

2. In another saucepan, melt chocolate chips on low to medium heat until melted. Stir constantly to prevent them from burning. Remove from heat when fully melted.

3. In a food processor, pulse together the ricotta cheese, tofu, cream cheese, and salt. Once combined thoroughly, add in the dissolved sugar, melted chocolate, and agar-agar powder. Blend until completely smooth. Taste and adjust accordingly.

4. Pour the chocolate ricotta cheesecake mixture into the cooled crust. Bake for 25 to 30 minutes or until the pie has set. Allow to cool fully on cooling rack. Then refrigerate at least 4 hours before serving.

Toast remaining ¾ cup pine nuts in the oven until they are deep gold color. Sprinkle the toasted pine nuts on the pie while they are both still warm.

Banana cream pie is straight up special to me. That was the chosen pie my family would get when Marie Callender's was having their pie sale. Luckily for me, the pies would go in the garage fridge. I, already becoming a sugar savage, would sneak into that fridge with a hidden spoon and go to banana cream pie town. No one ever caught me. My banana cream pie recipe is an homage to my younger self. It tastes just like—if not better—than the pie I grew up eating.

Buy bananas a few days ahead of time so that when you use them they're ripe. They should have lots of brown speckles and be borderline mushy. If you want to make this recipe today, then I suggest buying super ripe bananas from your local gas station/convenience store. Their produce is always kinda old! You should also have some perfectly ripe, non-mushy bananas for the slices.

Crust:
1 ¼ cup all-purpose flour
½ teaspoon sugar
¼ teaspoon salt
3-4 tablespoon ice-cold water
½ cup v. butter, chopped into
  cubes and froze for 5 minutes

Filling:
1 cup canned coconut milk
½ cup soymilk
1 cup sugar
1 ½ very ripe bananas, plus 2
  bananas sliced
1 package Mori-Nu Extra Firm
  Silken Tofu*
½ cup + 3 tablespoon cornstarch
¼ teaspoon salt
2 tablespoon v. butter
1 teaspoon vanilla extract
1 teaspoon banana extract

Topping:
v. whipped cream*
banana, sliced

Specialty ingredient buy ahead

CRUST

1. Prepare crust first. In a medium bowl, whisk together the flour, sugar, and salt.

2. Add in the cold butter cubes. Incorporate butter into flour my using your fingers, or by pulsing a few times in a food processor. Mix until it becomes course meal.

3. Add in ice water 1 tablespoon at a time. Stop adding water when the dough comes together. You want to steer clear of wet dough and dough that easily falls apart, you want a happy medium.

4. Knead the dough once or twice, then shape into a ball and wrap in plastic wrap. Store in the fridge for 2 days or overnight.

5. Preheat oven to 375. Get your pie tin out.

6. Using a rolling pin, roll the dough out on a flat surface lightly coated in flour. Roll into the best circle you can make. Gently pick up the dough and place on the pie tin. Press and pinch til pretty and smooth.

7. Put a sheet of aluminum paper over the pie dough, and then spread pie weights over the foil. This will prevent the dough from bubbling up. Cook the dough for 16-20 minutes, or until the edges are nice and golden.

8. While the pie crust is cooling, prepare the banana cream filling.

FILLING

1. In a medium saucepan, stir together the cornstarch, sugar, and salt. Whisk in the coconut milk and soymilk and stir constantly for about 5 minutes on medium heat. It'll start to thicken pretty rapidly, eventually becoming a pudding paste. Remove from heat when it's at this point.

2. In a food processor, blend the tofu with the bananas until smooth. Add in the pudding paste, vanilla extract, banana extract, and melted butter. Blend until smooth.

3. If the mixture doesn't seem light enough, add in more soymilk. Just be aware that the filling should be the consistency of thick pudding, you know, cream pie! Sometimes the sweetness of the bananas are unpredictable, so, if needed, add in some maple syrup too. Adjust accordingly, then blend.

4. Slice bananas and line the bottom of the pie crust with them. Pour the banana cream filling over. Refrigerate overnight.

Before serving, spread whipped cream over the pie. Add banana slices to the edges.

COOKIES'N'MILK PIE

When I eat chocolate chip cookies fresh outta the oven, I drop the cookie in a huge mug of soymilk and let it soak, then proceed. I like my milk with some cookies. This pie is perfect for someone like me. You still get plenty of the chocolate chip cookie goodness while the milk part is already done for you. I originally served this at Los Angeles Vegan Beer & Food Festival as a secret menu item and it was literally sold out in seconds. Make this and sell it out yourself by eating it all.

CRUST

1. In an electric mixer using the whisk attachment, beat the butter with the sugars for 3 minutes.

2. While the butter and sugars are mixing, combine the flour, baking soda, and salt in a separate bowl.

3. Once the butter and sugars are light and fluffy, add in applesauce and vanilla extract. Beat until combined.

4. Switch the whisk attachment to the paddle attachment or use a rubber spatula and some elbow grease. Add the flour, baking soda, and salt mixture to the wet mixture. Mix until combined. Gently fold in chocolate chips.

5. Press the cookie dough onto pie tin, evenly. Place in freezer for about an hour.

6. Bake cookie dough crust at 350 degrees for about 15 minutes, or until golden. Place on cooling rack.

Crust:
1 ¾ cup all-purpose flour
½ cup sugar
½ cup brown sugar
½ cup v. butter, melted
¼ cup applesauce
1 tablespoon vanilla
½ teaspoon baking soda
½ teaspoon salt
½ cup chocolate chips*

Milk pudding filling:
1 cup canned coconut
  milk
½ cup soymilk
⅓ cup sugar
2 tablespoon + 1
  teaspoon cornstarch
⅛ teaspoon salt
1 teaspoon v. butter
1 teaspoon vanilla extract

*Specialty ingredient
  buy ahead*

FILLING

1. In a medium saucepan, whisk the sugar, cornstarch, and salt together.

2. Stir in the coconut and soymilk on medium heat for about 6 minutes, whisking constantly. Once it's thickened and reached a pudding-like consistency, remove from heat and add butter and vanilla extract.

3. Pour milk pudding into the cookie crust. Refrigerate for a few hours or overnight before serving.

PIES

EVERYDAY BAKING MIX

If you're feeling too casual or shy to dance, the Everyday Baking Mix is your friend. It's the perfect mix to put on if you have a baking partner over who isn't much of dancer, more of a listener. Put them on whisking duty and turn the volume uuuup!

claracakes..com

"10:15 Saturday Night" — The Cure
"Corporeal" — Broadcast
"Life & Death" — Chairmen Of The Board
"Miss Modular"— Stereolab
"Shadow of a Doubt" — Sonic Youth
"The Goldheart Mountaintop
  Queen Directory" — Guided by Voices
"Tears Dry on Their Own" — Amy Winehouse
"For the Sake of the Song" — Townes Van Zandt
"Streets of Bakersfield" — Buck Owens
"Do What You Gotta Do" — Nina Simone
"Didn't Cha Know" — Erykah Badu
"Jay Dee 10" — J Dilla
"Pick Up the Change" — Wilco
"Strawberry Letter 23" — Shuggie Otis
"Your Heart Out" — The Fall
"Southern Nights" — Allen Toussaint
"Hang on to Your Love" — Sade
"Impatient" — Jeremih

CHAPTER 5
FROSTINGS

Historically, frosting isn't my favorite. I'm the person that scrapes frosting off a cupcake to enjoy what is basically a muffin at that point. However, this is not the case with the frosting I make.

In this world, most frosting out there is thick, overly sugary, grainy, or oily. When I say this to myself I think, "What?!" It's no wonder I disliked it for so long! So, when I started making cakes, frosting came easy to me because I knew exactly what I wanted out of it. Frosting needs to be light, almost whipped-cream like. It needs to be completely smooth, *like butt-ah*. And it needs to be just sweet enough to compliment the cake, nothing more, nothing less.

These frosting recipes have been tested on many, many people who had a bad impression of frosting that was then changed—including me. My fellow frosting haters, this one's for you.

Make sure to have lots of soap and hot water on hand when you make this, because frosting will probably get all over your hands, making you a bit slimy and uncomfortable.

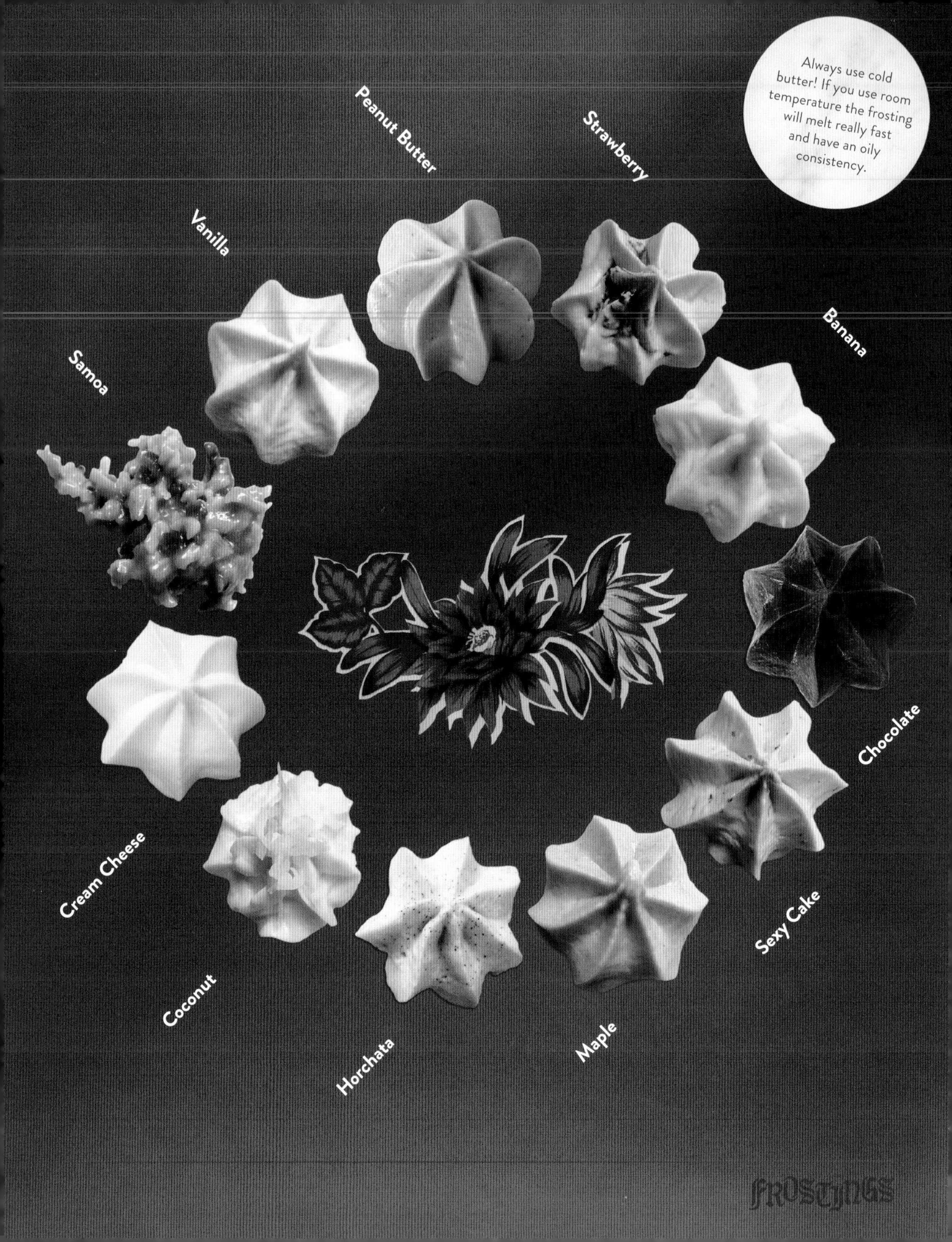
Always use cold butter! If you use room temperature the frosting will melt really fast and have an oily consistency.
Peanut Butter
Strawberry
Vanilla
Banana
Samoa
Chocolate
Cream Cheese
Sexy Cake
Coconut
Maple
Horchata
FROSTINGS

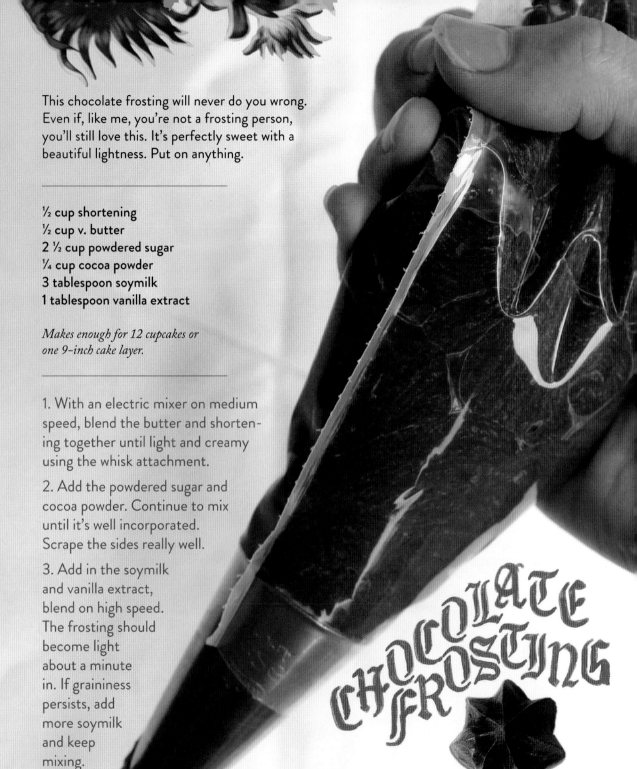

This chocolate frosting will never do you wrong. Even if, like me, you're not a frosting person, you'll still love this. It's perfectly sweet with a beautiful lightness. Put on anything.

½ cup shortening
½ cup v. butter
2 ½ cup powdered sugar
¼ cup cocoa powder
3 tablespoon soymilk
1 tablespoon vanilla extract

Makes enough for 12 cupcakes or one 9-inch cake layer.

---

1. With an electric mixer on medium speed, blend the butter and shortening together until light and creamy using the whisk attachment.

2. Add the powdered sugar and cocoa powder. Continue to mix until it's well incorporated. Scrape the sides really well.

3. Add in the soymilk and vanilla extract, blend on high speed. The frosting should become light about a minute in. If graininess persists, add more soymilk and keep mixing.

CHOCOLATE FROSTING

This frosting is like Ben and Jerry's Chunky Monkey ice cream meets whipped cream meets vanilla frosting. Eat with a spoon or make a cake for it.

½ cup mashed bananas
½ cup shortening
¼ cup v. butter
2 ½-3 cup powdered sugar
1 teaspoon vanilla extract
½ teaspoon banana extract
½ teaspoon lemon juice
1 tablespoon soymilk

Makes enough for 12 cupcakes or one 9-inch cake layer.

1. Using an electric mixer with the whisk attachment, mix together the butter and shortening until smooth, on medium speed. Mix in banana until completely incorporated.

2. Add in powdered sugar and mix until smooth. Make sure to scrape the sides of the bowl.

3. Mix in the extracts, lemon juice, and soymilk. Mix on medium speed until the frosting is smooth and light. If it's grainy, add a little more soymilk and mix on high speed.

BANANA FROSTING

Nothing complements a spiced cake quite like cream cheese frosting. The lemon juice in this recipe gives it a subtle tanginess to enhance the cream cheese flavor more. Using shortening prevents the cream cheese and butter from melting into a sugary puddle.

½ cup v. cream cheese*
¼ cup shortening
¼ cup v. butter
2 ½ cup powdered sugar
1 teaspoon vanilla extract
1 teaspoon lemon juice

Makes enough for 12 cupcakes or one 9-inch cake layer.
* Specialty ingredient buy ahead

1. Using an electric mixer, mix together the cream cheese, shortening, and butter until smooth, on medium speed.

2. Slowly mix in the powdered sugar until smooth. Scrape down sides of the bowl.

3. Add in the vanilla extract and lemon juice. Mix until completely smooth and light on medium speed.

CREAM CHEESE FROSTING

MAPLE FROSTING

I love breakfast foods, so it's only natural that I lean towards maple frosting over vanilla. It's got a flare to it that compliments anything banana, caramel, or peanut butter related. Maple lifts ultra-rich foods and gives them the break they need!

½ cup shortening
½ cup v. butter
2 cup powdered sugar
¼ cup maple syrup
1 tablespoon vanilla extract
1 teaspoon maple extract (optional)

Makes enough for 12 cupcakes or one 9-inch cake layer.

1. Using an electric mixer with the whisk attachment, blend the butter and shortening together until light and creamy, on medium speed.

2. Add the maple syrup. Mix until it's well incorporated. Scrape the sides really well.

3. Add the powdered sugar until thoroughly mixed.

4. Add in the vanilla extract, and if using, the maple extract and blend on high speed. Mix until light and fluffy. The maple syrup in this may cause the frosting to melt faster, so make sure to keep refrigerated.

COCONUT FROSTING

For a while, I was always hesitant to make coconut frosting because it seemed like a vegan frosting cop out. Then I pulled myself out of that silly funk when I realized coconut frosting is really popular in general, and delicious. This recipe rules because of the combination of butter, shortening, and coconut oil. It's sturdy, while still having the coconut decadence. You can mix coconut shreds in but I would sprinkle them on the frosting after decorating instead to make the frosting more spreadable.

¼ cup v. butter
¼ cup solid coconut oil (store in refrigerator for a couple hours before use if it's hot outside)
¼ cup shortening
2-2 ½ cup powdered sugar
1 tablespoon vanilla extract
1 splash soymilk

Makes enough for 12 cupcakes or one 9-inch cake layer.

1. On medium speed using an electric mixer with the whisk attachment, blend the coconut oil, butter, and shortening together until light and creamy.

2. Add the powdered sugar until thoroughly mixed.

3. Add in the vanilla extract and soymilk. Mix until light and fluffy.

PEANUT BUTTER FROSTING

Peanut butter frosting seems like bold flavor, but it compliments everything from banana to maple to chocolate cake! You can go for a peanut butter cup flavor combo, a banana coconut bacon combo, or even a pb&j combo! It's basic in the best way possible.

½ cup v. butter
¼ cup natural, smooth peanut butter (if using one that you have to stir, refrigerate one hour prior to use)
2-2 ½ cup powdered sugar
1 teaspoon vanilla extract
1 splash soymilk

Makes enough for 12 cupcakes or one 9-inch cake layer.

1. Using an electric mixer with the whisk attachment on medium speed, blend the peanut butter and butter together until fully incorporated. Make sure to scrape the sides of the bowl.

2. Add the powdered sugar and mix until smooth.

3. Add in vanilla extract and soymilk and mix until frosting is light and fluffy. If graininess persists, add more soymilk and mix on high.

SAMOA FROSTING

If frosting is too thick, add a splash or two of soymilk and stir so that it's spreadable.

This frosting is very similar to German chocolate frosting, but it has extra coconut and no pecans. The coconut is also toasted to perfection because if you're not toasting coconut each time you use it are you really living?

2 ½ cup toasted, flaked coconut
1 cup brown sugar
½ cup coconut milk

¾ cup soymilk
½ tablespoon vanilla extract
3 tablespoon cornstarch
½ teaspoon salt

Makes enough for 12 cupcakes or one 9-inch cake layer.

1. In a small bowl, whisk together the soymilk and cornstarch. Set aside.

2. In a medium saucepan over medium heat, whisk the brown sugar into the coconut milk until the mixture boils. Lower the temperature and cook for 5 minutes, it should thicken.

3. Add the soymilk and cornstarch and salt slowly to the brown sugar-milk mixture on low heat, stirring constantly until the mixture is very thick. Turn off heat and add in the vanilla until completely mixed in. Stir in the toasted coconut. Store in refrigerator and allow to cool before using.

VANILLA FROSTING

I've never been a huge fan of frosting. Growing up, I'd scrape off about two thirds of the frosting on a cupcake, leaving more of a slather of frosting-butter. Most of the frosting was too thick, too sweet, and too chalky. Nowadays, frosting is something I take great pride in. I keep it light, just sweet enough, and slightly salty to give the cake extra flavor.

1. Using an electric mixer with the whisk attachment, cream together the shortening and butter on high speed until completely smooth.

2. On medium speed, add in the powdered sugar. Mix until smooth, making sure to scrape sides of the bowl.

3. Add in the vanilla extract and soymilk. Mix on high speed for about a minute, or until any graininess is mixed away. If graininess persists, add more soymilk and mix on high.

shortening
butter
powdered
tablespoon vanilla
extract
3 tablespoon soymilk

Makes enough for 12 cupcakes or one 9-inch cake layer.

Horchata frosting is a key component to Horchata cake (pg. 128). It seals the deal of the cake and pudding with it's sweet lightness and additional cinnamon spice. You could probably even drink this if you wanted to, but it might take longer to finish than a regular horchata.

HORCHATA FROSTING

1. In an electric mixer, cream together the butter and shortening on medium speed. Blend until completely creamy, making sure to scrape down the sides of the bowl.

2. Add in powdered sugar, horchata, and vanilla. Mix on highest speed, again, taking breaks to scrape down the sides of the bowl. Blend until smooth and light.

Make Horchata in advance. See page 53.

½ cup v. butter
⅓ cup shortening
2 cup powdered sugar
¼ cup horchata (pg. 53)
1 teaspoon vanilla extract

Makes enough for 12 cupcakes or one 9-inch cake layer.

SEXY CAKE FROSTING

Make sexy sauce in advance! See page 54.

This frosting is my answer to how to complete a cake when it's a hot LA day. It's light, playful, and exactly the sorta tangy sweetness you'd want to temporarily escape from the heat. I use this on the sexy cake (pg. 142).

½ cup shortening
½ cup v. butter
2 ½ cup powdered sugar
4 tablespoon key lime juice
1 teaspoon vanilla extract
¼ cup sexy sauce (pg. 54)

Makes enough for 12 cupcakes or one 9-inch cake layer.

1. Using an electric mixer with the whisk attachment blend the butter and shortening together until light and creamy on medium speed.

2. Add the powdered sugar and key lime juice. Mix until it's well incorporated. Scrape the sides really well.

3. Add in the vanilla extract, blend on high speed. The frosting should become light about a minute in. Using a spatula, gently fold in the sexy sauce.

STRAWBERRY FROSTING

First off, I'm sorry that I don't use actual strawberries in this recipe. At the beginning of the game, I did. Using fresh strawberries resulted in really runny, messy frosting. As a result, I sold my soul and figured strawberry extract makes for a much more delicious and pleasant frosting. Save the fresh strawberries for the strawberry cake (p. 110) and to decorate the frosting with!

1. Using an electric mixer with the whisk attachment on medium speed, cream together the shortening and butter.

2. Add in powdered sugar, soymilk, strawberry extract, vanilla extract, and red food coloring. Mix on medium, then crank it up all the way to high to mix out any graininess. Add soymilk about a teaspoon at a time and speed up if it's too thick or grainy.

½ cup v. butter
½ cup shortening
2-2 ½ cup powdered sugar
2-3 tablespoon soymilk
1 teaspoon vanilla extract
1 teaspoon strawberry extract
2 drops red food coloring

Makes enough for 12 cupcakes or one 9-inch cake layer.

BREAKING EVEN

When I was little, I was the girl getting the neighborhood kids together to run a lemonade stand. So, when I got my first cake orders, and through them my first taste of the baking business, I was hooked.

The thing I want to emphasize here is how much harder—and stronger—my business is because I've had to think through every event I've sold at, in advance, to ensure I make my money back. When you run your own company, especially a food service business, you are constantly gambling.

I learned this when I first started hosting pop-ups at Thank You For Coming. Thank You For Coming is a food and art space based in the Los Angeles neighborhood Atwater Village. The amazing collective that runs it invites artists and community members to experiment with food projects. I have been lucky enough to host a dinner, and a few diner-themed breakfasts there.

I remember being at the check-out at Restaurant Depot, a wholesale restaurant supplier, and looking at four

digits before the decimal when they rang me up! You swipe your card, pack your car up, and promote the heck out of your event and make sure it's special enough that people will come back a second and third time.

I realize how much of a struggle it can be for a working class person to start running a business. My personal advice is this:

• Price your services to completely cover your costs and then some. Not only is the product you are providing important, but your time is totally valuable, too.

• Try to calculate exactly how many products you need, so you don't overbuy. Guess according to social media RSVPs. If you sell out, that's much better than having leftover food!

• Save your receipts since you might be able to return things you haven't used.

• Give this investment your all. You'll only have this moment in time with the people that show up. Make it special for everyone, and hopefully they'll remember you, or at least the good experience.

CHAPTER 6
CAKES
and
CUPCAKES

*A*h yes. Here we are. The cake chapter. The cake chapter is home base for you and I. If you have had one of my cakes before, you should be able to taste how specific my cake preferences are. The proper cake is moist, it's light, it's not overly sweet, and it's salted just enough.

Cakes and cupcakes are what I have been best known for over the past few years. I sell them to a few different restaurants around LA because of how perfectly convenient they are. I pack as much love and flavor into each one of those little liners as possible.

I make cakes and cupcakes to win people over. Business meeting? Bring a cupcake. If I want a shop to carry my desserts? Bring a cupcake. I even made avocado cupcakes for an avocado themed competition, and I won an award for it (and a super sharp knife I use to this day)! Bring cupcakes!

There are thousands of different cake, frosting, and filling combos that run through my head. For me, I'm never really satisfied with myself when I just bake some simple chocolate/vanilla cupcakes. You will know I'm extremely busy if you buy a cupcake of mine and it is chocolate/vanilla (even though they're also very delicious). The recipes here are for some of my experimental favorites and the tried-and-true, best-selling ones. They go beyond simply satisfying a sweet tooth, to bring your taste buds together and reward them all at once.

HOW TO BUILD A CLARA CAKE

So, I've got all these recipes for you to bake a decked out cake or cupcake. But, you're probably wondering how to piece the cake, filling, and frosting components together. Here's a guide to help you with that:

Cake layers:

To make an entire cake you will need two (2) cake layers. A bottom layer and a top layer (with filling in between). The cake recipes in this chapter are for a single 9-inch layer, so double the ingredients when grocery shopping to make sure you get enough to make a complete cake!

No sticking!:

Trace a 9-inch, round cake pan on parchment paper. Cut it out. Do this twice (one time for each cake layer). Spray two (2) 9-inch round cake pans with nonstick spray. Then coat with a thin layer of flour. Then place a parchment paper circle inside each pan. This allows for the cake to come free without sticking to the pan.

Taking the cake out of the pan:

1. Gently place a butter knife between the cake edge and the pan. Slowly scrape along the edge of the cake pan, in order to ensure that the edge of the cake does not stick.

2. Take two cooling racks out. Spray with nonstick spray and dust with flour. This ensures that the cake won't stick to the wire on the cooling rack.

3. Place one cooling rack, bottom up, on top of cake pan, so that the cooling rack completely covers the top of the cake pan. Grip the cake pan while also holding the cooling rack against it. Slowly flip the cooling rack and cake pan onto a table surface, so that the cake slowly comes out of pan and onto the cooling rack. Remove cake pan from cake layer, and slowly peel parchment paper off of the cake. Do this for both cake layers.

4. Allow cake layers to cool for one hour. If the middle of the cake is still warm against the back of your palm, let cool longer. If you rush this step the frosting will melt right off the cake! Don't do that! You've come too far!

Pick your cake plate carefully:

Deciding what you're going to serve this cake on is crucial. It's impossible to transfer a cake all beautifully frosted onto a different plate, or off of a cake board, without making a mess.

If you're traveling with it, and don't know what plate it'll be on, use a 12-inch cake board. (I prefer greaseproof.) This is very handy since you can place the cake in a cake box without weighing it down.

If you know what you're serving the cake on, and aren't traveling with the cake, place the cake directly on that plate or cake stand. This way, when you cut into the cake you won't see an unnecessary, cake board. It'll just be a beautiful plate! You know?

Assembling cake:

1. Place the top of the plate or cake board directly on top of the cake layer. Try to center the plate or cake board so that the cake will be in the center.

2. While holding the plate/board against the top of the cake, also grip the cooling rack. Flip over so that the plate is now bottom-down on a surface, and the cake is on top of the plate. Slowly remove cooling rack off of cake, to ensure it doesn't rip a large chunk off.

3. Grab your filling and spread it evenly on top of the cake, leave a 2-inch border around the cake so that filling doesn't spill out when the top cake layer is placed on top of it. This is your only chance to fill up the middle of the cake, so it do it up big!

4. Grab the second cake layer/cooling rack. Pick up both sides of the cooling rack, centering it over the bottom cake layer. Carefully flip cooling rack over so that the cake slowly comes off and lies perfectly atop the filling layer.

Frosting the cake:

I'm not overly particular about how my cakes are frosted. I mainly want the cake's frosting to be as smooth as can be. For that, I use a frosting spatula. You can get one at most craft stores. It makes all the difference because it doesn't leave indent marks like a butter knife. I also like to pipe flowers around the bottom and top of the cake.

1. If you baked a chocolate cake, you want to do a crumb coat first. This will help you avoid seeing a bunch of dark crumbs in the frosting.

2. Scoop about a ¼-⅓ of your frosting into a bowl to avoid crumb contamination.

3. Using the smaller amount of frosting, frost a thin layer on the entire cake. Place in the fridge for about 20 minutes.

4. After 20 minutes, or if using a lighter colored cake, continue frosting the rest of the cake as evenly as possible.

5. Once the entire cake is frosted, get a paper towel damp and clean the rim of the cake board or plate.

6. Using whatever nozzle and pastry bag you please, pipe flowers or stars or whatever your heart desires around the top and bottom borders of the cake.

7. If traveling with the cake, box your cake up and place in fridge. If keeping cake at home, still be sure to place it in the fridge.

8. Take cake out of fridge and slice it. Allow it to sit for 30 minutes before eating so that it's nice and soft when you serve it.

Topping cakes:

Topping cakes and cupcakes is the easiest step of construction. It is the cherry on top. For toppings I prefer thinly sliced strawberries, or fragments of other non-sliceable fruit, like raspberries.

If topping a cake with nuts, I urge you to toast them in butter before! It deepens the flavor so much more, and will really bring out the sweetness of the cake.

If you're topping a cake or cupcakes with chocolate ganache, and want that zig zag effect, use a squeeze bottle. You can find them at any market for around two bucks. It will take your sweets to another level of classiness and is much easier to use than a spoon!

HOW TO BUILD A CLARA CAKE
CUPCAKE EDITION

Your cupcakes are all laid out on a cooling rack, waiting to be filled. The question is, "How do you pack as much as you can into these little guys?" Here's how!

1. If you're filling the cupcakes, fill them before frosting. If you're using a pudding filling, you can pipe the filling using a Wilton 230 tip and pastry bag. Just insert the tip directly into the center of the cupcake and squeeze bag to release filling.

2. If you're filling the cupcakes with a berry sauce, or something less smooth than pudding, you should manually cut small circles out of the center of each cupcake. Using a knife, cut a somewhat deep hole, from the top down, but make sure to leave enough cake to cover the bottom of the liner. Scoop the cake hole out.

3. Add about 1½–2 tablespoons worth of filling into each cupcake.

4. You can frost cupcakes using a frosting spatula, or pipe frosting using a pastry bag and tip. I prefer piping frosting since it takes less time. I opt for 12-inch plastic, disposable pastry bags and larger tips for a nice frosting swirl.

5. A great trick for filling the pastry bag that I was taught, is to place the pastry bag (with the tip already inserted ready to go) inside a wide-mouth cup. Wrap the top of the pastry bag over the edges of the cup, opening the bag up. Then, using a rubber spatula, scoop frosting into the bag about two-thirds of the way full. Remove bag by grabbing the edges and close it. Gently squeeze the frosting to make sure the air bubbles are out.

6. Slow and steady is the key to piping frosting. Just think about frosting a swirl because that's ultimately what you're doing!

CAKES

VANILLA CAKE

I remember in the sixth grade, after I got home from a really awkward ballet class, I attempted to make vanilla cupcakes and they nearly brought me to tears because they tasted so strange. Way different than what vanilla cake-box cakes had tasted like. What I learned from that is to always use butter in vanilla cake recipes. Oil-based vanilla cake just tastes like baked oil and vanilla which is no match for a sensitive sixth grader's taste buds. Eventually, I perfected the cake box inspired recipe. I quit ballet within a couple weeks.

Vanilla cake:
1 ¼ cup all-purpose flour
¾ cup sugar
½ cup coconut milk
½ cup soymilk
½ cup v. butter
1 tablespoon coconut vinegar
½ tablespoon baking powder
2 teaspoon vanilla extract

Makes 12 cupcakes or one 9-inch cake layer. Double recipe for complete cake!

1. Preheat oven to 350 degrees. Line a muffin pan with 12 cupcake liners or trace a 9-inch round cake pan on parchment paper with a pencil. Cut the circle out. Coat the cake pan with nonstick spray and flour and place parchment paper circle on top.

2. Whisk the coconut milk, soymilk, and vinegar together until slightly foamy. Set aside.

3. While the milk and vinegar mixture is curdling, cream together the butter and sugar in an electric mixer using the whisk attachment. Mix on medium speed until light and fluffy. Scrape down sides of the bowl every once in awhile. Sugar granules will still remain, but that's okay.

4. Add vanilla extract to the butter and sugar and mix until it's fully incorporated.

5. In a separate bowl, sift the flour and baking powder together.

6. Gradually add in the flour mixture and the milk mixture to the butter sugar mixture. Mix everything until smooth. Make sure that you scrape any buttery chunks you see into the middle of the bowl so you can smooth that sucker out.

7. Using an ice cream scoop, scoop batter into cupcake liners.

OR

If using a cake pan, pour batter into pan. Scrape all the batter out of the bowl using a rubber spatula. Even out the batter by moving the pan back and forth.

For complete cake construction instructions see page 92. CAKES

8. Bake cupcakes 18 minutes or until toothpick comes out clean when poked in a cupcake. Transfer to cooling rack.

OR

Bake cake for 25 minutes or until a toothpick comes out clean when poked in the center of the cake.

9. To take the cake out, place a cooling rack on top of cake so the tiny legs are sticking up and not towards the cake, then flip the cooling rack and pan altogether, place on a surface, and remove the cake pan and parchment paper, slowly. Allow to fully cool before frosting.

Use vanilla frosting for both filling and frosting.

VANILLA FROSTING

1. Using an electric mixer with the whisk attachment, cream together the shortening and butter on high speed until completely smooth.

2. On medium speed, add in the powdered sugar. Mix until smooth, making sure to scrape sides of the bowl.

3. Add in the vanilla extract and soymilk. Mix on high speed for about a minute, or until any graininess is mixed away. If graininess persists, add more soymilk and mix on high.

Vanilla frosting:
½ cup shortening
½ cup v. butter
2 ½ cup powdered sugar
1 tablespoon vanilla
 extract
3 tablespoons soymilk

Makes enough frosting for 12 cupcakes or one 9-inch cake layer. Triple recipe for 2-layer frosting and filling.

CHOCOLATE CAKE

During WWII, there was a ration on basic foods such as eggs and butter. As a result, people had to get creative when baking a cake since each person had an allowance of just one egg a week. When vinegar is combined with a milk, it creates buttermilk, while also becoming an egg substitute. It's what gives this cake the fluffiness and light texture that an egg would. I'm not sure who was the first to figure out that vinegar could substitute eggs in a recipe, but I'm forever grateful.

1. Preheat oven to 350 degrees. Line a muffin pan with 12 cupcake liners.

OR

Preheat oven to 350 degrees. Trace a 9-inch round cake pan on parchment paper with a pencil. Cut the circle out. Coat the cake pan with nonstick spray and flour and place parchment paper circle on top.

2. Using a whisk, mix the soymilk, coconut milk, and coconut vinegar in large bowl. Set aside.

3. While the buttermilk mixture is curdling, sift together the flour, cocoa powder, baking soda, baking powder, and salt in a medium bowl.

4. Add the sugar, canola oil, and vanilla extract to the buttermilk mixture. Whisk for about 2 minutes. The mixture should be slightly foamy.

5. Add the sifted ingredients to the wet. Mix until smooth, but be sure not to mix beyond that. Otherwise, you might have dense cake on your hands!

6. Using an ice cream scooper, fill cupcake liners about ⅔ of the way full. Bake for 18 minutes or until a toothpick comes out clean. Transfer to cooling rack. Frost cupcakes when completely cooled.

OR

Bake cake for 25 minutes or until a toothpick comes out clean when poked in the center of the cake.

7. To take the cake out, place a cooling rack on top of cake so the tiny legs are sticking up and not towards the cake, then flip the cooling rack and pan altogether, place on a surface, and remove the cake pan and parchment paper, slowly. Allow to fully cool before frosting.

Use vanilla frosting for both filling and frosting.

Chocolate cake:
1 cup all-purpose flour
½ cup soymilk
½ cup coconut milk
¾ cup sugar
½ cup canola oil
⅓ cup cocoa powder
½ tablespoon coconut vinegar
1 tablespoon vanilla extract
¼ teaspoon salt
¾ teaspoon baking soda
1 teaspoon baking powder

Makes 12 cupcakes or one 9-inch cake layer. Double recipe for complete cake!

VANILLA FROSTING

1. Using an electric mixer with the whisk attachment, cream together the shortening and butter on high speed until completely smooth.

2. On medium speed, add in the powdered sugar. Mix until smooth, making sure to scrape sides of the bowl.

3. Add in the vanilla extract and soymilk. Mix on high speed for about a minute, or until any graininess is mixed away. If graininess persists, add more soymilk and mix on high.

Vanilla frosting:
½ cup shortening
½ cup v. butter
2 ½ cup powdered sugar
1 tablespoon vanilla extract
3 tablespoon soymilk

Makes enough frosting for 12 cupcakes or one 9-inch cake layer. Triple recipe for 2-layer frosting and filling.

Truth be told, for a long while I stayed away from making coconut flavored anything. I always thought coconut cake was such a vegan cop-out, but I got over that when I realized coconut cake is a classic flavor across the whole dang board. I don't know how, but coconut products have a way of imbuing any dessert with a melt in your mouth quality.

This recipe is coconut packed. I found using only coconut milk results in basically a white cake flavor. This recipe uses coconut vinegar, coconut oil, coconut milk, and toasted coconut flakes. All your hard work will pay off when a friend eats a slice and says, "I love this coconut cake!" Instead of, "Yummy white cake!" Can you imagine? Luckily you won't have to!

CAKES

COCONUT CAKE

Toasted coconut:
2 cup flaked coconut
¼ cup melted coconut oil
½ teaspoon salt

Coconut cake:
1 cup canned coconut milk
1 ¼ cup all-purpose flour
1 cup toasted coconut flakes
¼ cup melted coconut oil
¼ cup v. butter, room temperature
¾ cup sugar
2 teaspoon vanilla extract
½ tablespoon coconut vinegar
1 tablespoon baking powder
1 teaspoon baking soda
¼ teaspoon salt

Makes 12 cupcakes or one 9-inch cake layer. Double recipe for complete cake!

1. Preheat oven to 350 degrees. Line a baking sheet with parchment paper.

2. In a large bowl, toss together the coconut flakes, coconut oil, and salt making sure the flakes are completely coated in the oil.

3. Spread the flakes over the parchment paper evenly and put in oven. Stir the coconut every couple of minutes to ensure the flakes bake evenly, about 7-8 minutes.

4. Let cool on pan, don't remove from pan until you need them for the cake since they get nice and crunchy on the pan. Before adding to cake batter, soak up excess oil with a paper towel.

COCONUT CAKE

1. Preheat oven to 350 degrees. Line a muffin pan with 12 cupcake liners.

OR

Preheat oven to 350 degrees. Trace a 9-inch round cake pan on parchment paper with a pencil. Cut the circle out. Coat the cake pan with nonstick spray and flour and place parchment paper circle on top.

2. In a large mixing bowl, whisk together the coconut milk and vinegar until foamy. Set aside while preparing the next steps.

3. In a medium mixing bowl, sift together the flour, baking powder, baking soda, and salt.

4. Using an electric mixer, mix the butter, coconut oil, and sugar on medium speed until light and fluffy.

5. Add vanilla extract to the butter and sugar mixture.

6. Add the dry ingredients and the coconut milk-vinegar to the butter. Mix on medium speed until no large clumps remain. Mix in the coconut flakes.

7. Using an ice cream scooper, fill cupcake liners about ⅔ of the way full. Bake for 18 minutes or until a toothpick comes out clean. Transfer to cooling rack. Frost cupcakes when completely cooled.

OR

Make sure that the canned coconut milk is room temperature. If you open the can and it's solidified, heat it up in a saucepan on low heat and whisk it until the liquid is evenly distributed.

Bake cake for 25 minutes or until a toothpick comes out clean when poked in the center of the cake.

8. To take the cake out, place a cooling rack on top of cake so the tiny legs are sticking up and not towards the cake, then flip the cooling rack and pan altogether, place on a surface, and remove the cake pan and parchment paper, slowly. Allow to fully cool before frosting.

Coconut frosting:
¼ cup v. butter
¼ cup solid coconut oil (store in refrigerator for a couple hours before use if it's hot outside)
½ cup shortening
2-2 ½ cup powdered sugar
1 tablespoon vanilla extract
1 splash soymilk

Makes enough frosting for 12 cupcakes or one 9-inch cake layer. Triple recipe for 2-layer frosting and filling.

Use coconut frosting for both filling and frosting.

COCONUT FROSTING

1. On medium speed using an electric mixer with the whisk attachment, blend the coconut oil, butter, and shortening together until light and creamy.

2. Add the powdered sugar until thoroughly mixed.

3. Add in the vanilla extract and soymilk. Mix until light and fluffy.

When I wrote this recipe I was kinda over using lemon extract. I use a fair amount of extracts, but lemon extract has always grossed me out. When using a citrus that is abundantly flavorful, it's a shame to rely on some watered down stuff in a bottle. As a result, this recipe relies on the lemon zest and lemon juice to really get that lemon punch in there. The sweetness combined with the zestiness of the lemon ingredients makes for a very addictive dessert since it's so well balanced.

CAKES

LEMON CAKE

1. Preheat oven to 350 degrees. Line a muffin pan with 12 cupcake liners.

OR

Preheat oven to 350 degrees. Trace a 9-inch round cake pan on parchment paper with a pencil. Cut the circle out. Coat the cake pan with nonstick spray and flour and place parchment paper circle on top.

2. In a large mixing bowl, whisk together the soymilk, coconut milk, and coconut vinegar until frothy. Set aside and prepare the next steps.

3. In a medium bowl, sift together the flour, baking soda, and baking powder.

4. Using an electric mixer with the whisk attachment, mix together the sugar and butter on medium speed until light and fluffy.

5. Add vanilla extract to sugar and butter at medium speed until well incorporated.

6. Whisk the lemon juice and lemon zest into the milk-vinegar mixture until completely combined.

Lemon cake:
1 ¼ cup all-purpose flour
1 cup sugar
½ cup soymilk
¼ cup canned coconut milk
1 teaspoon coconut vinegar
½ cup v. butter
3 tablespoon lemon zest
¼ cup lemon juice
1 teaspoon vanilla extract
½ teaspoon baking soda
1 teaspoon baking powder

Makes 12 cupcakes or one 9-inch cake layer. Double recipe for complete cake!

7. Add the wet and dry ingredients slowly to the butter-sugar mixture and mix on medium speed until just smooth. Make sure to scrape down the sides of the bowl every once in awhile.

8. Using an ice cream scooper, fill cupcake liners about ⅔ of the way full. Bake for 18 minutes or until a toothpick comes out clean. Transfer to cooling rack. Frost cupcakes when completely cooled.

OR

Bake cake for 25 minutes or until a toothpick comes out clean when poked in the center of the cake.

9. To take the cake out, place a cooling rack on top of cake so the tiny legs are sticking up and not towards the cake, then flip the cooling rack and pan altogether, place on a surface, and remove the cake pan and parchment paper, slowly. Allow to fully cool before frosting.

Use vanilla frosting for both filling and frosting.

VANILLA FROSTING

1. Using an electric mixer with the whisk attachment, cream together the shortening and butter on high speed until completely smooth.

2. On medium speed, add in the powdered sugar. Mix until smooth, making sure to scrape sides of the bowl.

3. Add in the vanilla extract and soymilk. Mix on high speed for about a minute, or until any graininess is mixed away. If graininess persists, add more soymilk and mix on high.

½ cup shortening
½ cup v. butter
2 ½ cup powdered sugar
1 tablespoon vanilla extract
3 tablespoon soymilk

Makes enough frosting for 12 cupcakes or one 9-inch cake layer. Triple recipe for 2-layer frosting and filling.

I suggest using a juicer to juice lemons. You can get a lot of bang for your buck this way! Zest lemons before juicing them, that way you're working with a dry, solid surface.

CAKES   For complete cake construction instructions see page 92.

STRAWBERRY CAKE

Strawberry cake is best prepared from April to June, which is strawberries' natural season.

I have very fond memories of strawberry cake, particularly strawberry mini-cupcakes. I remember back in the first grade, you could bring in a dessert of your choice on your birthday to share with the class. Strawberry cake was my chosen sweet. It was a cake box mix (with lots of extra love), topped with the strawberry frosting that you buy by the tub. I loved every lick of the frosting, and every bite of the cake—hated school.

This is gonna sound dramatic, but when I first made this cake I was taken aback a little. The frosting completely reminded me of the tub frosting, only way lighter, less grainy, and not overly sweet. I decided not to add any strawberry extract to the cake, and to depend on the flavor of fresh strawberries and strawberry jam. Boy, did they come through! This cake is perfectly light, moist, with the most beautiful, delicate sweetness and flavor of strawberries that no other fruit can really master as beautifully.

1. Preheat oven to 350 degrees. Line a muffin pan with 12 cupcake liners.

OR

Trace a 9-inch round cake pan on parchment paper with a pencil. Cut the circle out. Coat the cake pan with nonstick spray and flour and place parchment paper circle on top.

2. In a large mixing bowl, whisk the coconut milk, soymilk, and coconut vinegar together until frothy. Set aside and let curdle while you prep the next steps.

3. In a medium bowl, sift the flour, baking powder, and baking soda together.

4. Using an electric mixer with the whisk attachment, cream together sugar and butter on high speed. Once light and fluffy, add in vanilla extract and mix on medium speed until incorporated.

5. Add in the strawberry jam to the butter mixture and mix until completely blended in.

6. Add flour mixture and milk mixture into the butter

Strawberry cake:
1 ¼ cup all-purpose flour
½ cup soymilk
½ cup v. butter
¼ cup coconut milk
¼ cup strawberry preserves
⅓ cup strawberry skins, chopped
1 tablespoon coconut vinegar
½ tablespoon baking powder
½ tablespoon vanilla extract
¼ teaspoon baking soda

Makes 12 cupcakes or one 9-inch cake layer. Double recipe for complete cake!

mixture. Beat together on medium speed, making sure to scrape down the sides of the bowl every once in awhile. Beat until smooth. Very gently stir in the fresh strawberries until evenly distributed.

7. Scoop the batter into cupcake liners and bake for 18 minutes or until toothpick comes out clean when poked in the center.

OR

If using a cake pan, pour batter into pan. Scrape all the batter out of the bowl using a rubber spatula. Even out the batter by moving the pan back and forth. Bake for about 25 minutes.

8. Remove cupcakes from oven and transfer to a cooling rack. Allow to cool completely before frosting.

OR

To take the cake out, place a cooling rack on top of cake so the tiny legs are sticking up and not towards the cake, then flip the cooling rack and pan altogether, place on a surface, and remove the cake pan and parchment paper, slowly. Allow to fully cool before frosting.

Use strawberry frosting for both filling and frosting.

For complete cake construction instructions see page 92.   CAKES

STRAWBERRY FROSTING

1. Using an electric mixer with the whisk attachment on medium speed, cream together the shortening and butter.

2. Add in powdered sugar, soymilk, strawberry extract, vanilla extract, and red food coloring. Mix on medium, then crank it up all the way to high to mix out any graininess. Add soymilk about a teaspoon at a time and speed up if it's too thick or grainy.

½ cup v. butter
½ cup shortening
2-2 ½ cup powdered sugar
2-3 tablespoon soymilk
1 teaspoon vanilla extract
1 teaspoon strawberry extract
2 drops red food coloring

Makes enough frosting for 12 cupcakes or one 9-inch cake layer. Triple recipe for 2-layer frosting and filling.

While I love pumpkin bread, you can't just follow a pumpkin bread recipe, slap frosting on it, and call it a cake. It's just not the same. Here we have a light, fluffy, pumpkin cake that's got all the beautiful spices of the fall rainbow just waiting to be paired with some cream cheese frosting. Bake this into cupcakes or a cake, just please don't bake this cake batter in a loaf pan!

1. Preheat oven to 350 degrees. Line a muffin pan with 12 cupcake liners.

OR

Preheat oven to 350 degrees. Trace a 9-inch round cake pan on parchment paper with a pencil. Cut the circle out. Coat the cake pan with nonstick spray and flour and place parchment paper circle on top.

2. In a small cup, combine the soy milk and vinegar. Allow mixture to rest for 5 minutes.

3. In a large mixing bowl, mix together the flour, baking powder, baking soda, sugars, spices, and salt. Set aside.

4. Using an electric mixer, cream together the butter and sugars until creamy. Slowly add in the pumpkin puree, vanilla, and soymilk-vinegar mixture. Add the dry ingredients to the wet, mixing until just combined.

5. Using an ice cream scooper, fill cupcake liners about ⅔ of the way full. Bake for 18 minutes or until toothpick comes out clean. Transfer to cooling rack. Frost cupcakes when completely cooled.

OR

Bake cake for 25 minutes or until a toothpick comes out clean when poked in the center of the cake.

6. To take the cake out, place a cooling rack on top of cake so the tiny legs are sticking up and not towards the cake, then flip the cooling rack and pan altogether, place on a surface, and remove the cake pan and parchment paper, slowly. Allow to fully cool before frosting.

Pumpkin cake:
⅓ cup soy milk
1 ½ teaspoon coconut vinegar
1 ¼ cup all-purpose flour
1 tablespoon baking powder
½ tablespoon baking soda
½ cup brown sugar
¼ cup sugar
2 tablespoon ground cinnamon
½ tablespoon ginger
½ tablespoon nutmeg
½ teaspoon allspice
pinch of cloves
½ tablespoon salt
½ cup pumpkin puree
⅓ cup v. butter
2 teaspoon vanilla extract

Makes 12 cupcakes or one 9-inch cake layer. Double recipe for complete cake!

CAKES

Use cream cheese frosting for both filling and frosting.

CREAM CHEESE FROSTING

1. Using an electric mixer, mix together the cream cheese, shortening, and butter until smooth, on medium speed.

2. Slowly mix in the powdered sugar until smooth. Scrape down sides of the bowl.

3. Add in the vanilla extract and lemon juice. Mix until completely smooth and light on medium speed.

½ cup v. cream cheese*
¼ cup shortening
¼ cup v. butter
2 ½ cup powdered sugar
1 teaspoon vanilla extract
1 teaspoon lemon juice

Makes enough frosting for 12 cupcakes or one 9-inch cake layer. Triple recipe for 2-layer frosting and filling.

* Specialty ingredient buy ahead

PUMPKIN CAKE

MAPLE CAKE

In my book, maple is as beautiful a flavor as vanilla or chocolate. I love that it reminds me of breakfast, and therefore, I can eat maple cake for breakfast. The vanilla really brings out the maple flavor, and the use of dark brown sugar packs in a subtle molasses undertone while giving the cake a nice maple color. For some reason the idea of maple in a cake seems extra delicious because it feels like a step above pancakes.

Maple cake:
1 ½ cup all-purpose flour
½ cup dark brown sugar
½ cup maple syrup
½ cup soymilk
¼ cup coconut milk
½ cup v. butter
1 tablespoon vanilla
½ tablespoon coconut
  vinegar
½ tablespoon baking
  powder
¼ teaspoon baking soda

Makes 12 cupcakes or one 9-inch cake layer. Double recipe for complete cake!

1. Preheat oven to 350 degrees. Line a muffin pan with 12 cupcake liners.

OR

Preheat oven to 350 degrees. Trace a 9-inch round cake pan on parchment paper with a pencil. Cut the circle out. Coat the

cake pan with nonstick spray and flour and place parchment paper circle on top.

2. In a large mixing bowl, whisk together the soymilk, coconut milk, and vinegar until foamy. Set aside while you prepare the next steps.

3. In a medium bowl, sift together the flour, baking powder, and baking soda.

4. Using an electric mixer, cream together the sugar and butter until light and fluffy on medium to high speed.

5. Add vanilla extract to sugar and butter and mix until completely mixed in.

6. Add maple syrup and mix until incorporated.

7. Add the sifted dry ingredients and milk-vinegar mixture to the butter and beat on medium speed until batter is smooth. Make sure to scrape down sides of the bowl every once in awhile.

8. Using an ice cream scooper, fill cupcake liners about ⅔ of the way full. Bake for 18 minutes or until a toothpick comes out clean.

OR

Bake cake for 25 minutes or until a toothpick comes out clean when poked in the center of the cake.

9. To take the cake out, place a cooling rack on top of cake so the tiny legs are sticking up and not towards the cake, then flip the cooling rack and pan altogether, place on a surface, and remove the cake pan and parchment paper, slowly. Allow to fully cool before frosting.

MAPLE FROSTING

Use maple frosting for both filling and frosting.

1. Using an electric mixer with the whisk attachment, blend the butter and shortening together until light and creamy, on medium speed.

2. Add the maple syrup. Mix until it's well incorporated. Scrape the sides really well.

3. Add the powdered sugar until thoroughly mixed.

4. Add in the vanilla extract, and if using, the maple extract and blend on high speed. Mix until light and fluffy. The maple syrup in this may cause the frosting to melt faster, so make sure to keep refrigerated.

½ cup shortening
½ cup v. butter
2 cup powdered sugar
¼ cup maple syrup
1 teaspoon maple extract (optional)
1 tablespoon vanilla extract

Makes enough frosting for 12 cupcakes or one 9-inch cake layer. Triple recipe for 2-layer frosting and filling.

Hopefully I don't get a cease and desist letter in the mail from Ben and Jerry's because of this cupcake. To be fair, they *were* the number-one inspiration behind this cake flavor. Long before I was baking, my mom would eat cartons of Chunky Monkey ice cream while pregnant with my brothers and I. This cupcake is perfect for those cravings, and when you want something heartier than melty ice cream! But you don't have to be pregnant to eat them.

A helpful tip! In the perfect world, you'd buy bananas a week ahead so they get brown. If you're in a crunch, I highly recommend going to your local convenience store. If they have bananas, they are most likely very ripe.

CAKES

BANANA CAKE

1. Preheat oven to 350 degrees. Line a muffin pan with 12 cupcake liners.

OR

Preheat oven to 350 degrees. Trace a 9-inch round cake pan on parchment paper with a pencil. Cut the circle out. Coat the cake pan with nonstick spray and flour and place parchment paper circle on top.

2. In a blender, mix a banana on medium speed until smooth and liquidy.

3. Sift the flour, baking soda, baking powder, sugar, and salt in a medium sized bowl.

4. In a separate bowl, whisk together the butter, banana, soymilk, and extracts.

5. Add the wet ingredients to the dry ingredients and stir with a rubber spatula until just combined. Fold in the chocolate chips and walnuts.

6. Using an ice cream scooper, fill cupcake liners about ⅔ of the way full. Bake for 18 minutes or until a toothpick comes out clean. Transfer to cooling rack. Frost cupcakes when completely cooled.

OR

Bake cake for 25 minutes or until a toothpick comes out clean when poked in the center of the cake.

Banana cake:
1 ¼ cup all-purpose flour
1 cup sugar
½ cup soymilk
⅓ cup coconut milk
½ cup blended banana
   (use a very ripe banana)
½ cup melted v. butter
1 ¼ teaspoon baking
   powder
¼ teaspoon baking soda
1 teaspoon banana
   extract
1 tablespoon vanilla
   extract
½ cup chocolate chips*
¾ cup walnuts, chopped

Toppings:
walnuts, toasted
chocolate chips*

Makes 12 cupcakes or one 9-inch cake layer. Double recipe for complete cake!

CAKES

7. To take the cake out, place a cooling rack on top of cake so the tiny legs are sticking up and not towards the cake, then flip the cooling rack and pan altogether, place on a surface, and remove the cake pan and parchment paper, slowly. Allow to fully cool before frosting.

Use banana frosting for both filling and frosting.

BANANA FROSTING

1. In an electric mixer, blend the butter and shortening together on medium speed. Once creamed together, mix in the blended banana. When the banana is thoroughly mixed in, add the powdered sugar, vanilla and banana extracts, and soymilk. If the frosting looks too grainy, increase the speed to the highest setting and add in a couple more soymilk splashes.

Sprinkle chocolate chips and walnuts over entire cake.

Banana frosting:
½ cup shortening
½ cup v. butter
¼ cup blended banana
2 cup powdered sugar
1 tablespoon vanilla
  extract
1 teaspoon banana
  extract
splash of soymilk

Makes enough frosting for 12 cupcakes or one 9-inch cake layer. Triple recipe for 2-layer frosting and filling.

BREAKFAST CAKE

I'm sure you can imagine how many cakes I eat a day. Honestly, my standards for a delicious cake are really high now. There's a whole mental checklist I have when I eat any sweet, so it's gotta be a reaaaaally yummy cake to take me to dreamland and forget all about my work. This cake does just that for me.

Breakfast cake goes like this: Bake a banana cake, stuff it with maple "milk" pudding, frost it with milky, maple frosting, and coat it with caramelized, cornmeal-coated corn flakes. This cake has soul. The moist, bold, banana cake leads you into the milky, maple-ey, light pudding, getting you ready for the crunchy corn flake bite followed by a perfectly sweet wave of maple milk frosting to wash it away. I'd say one slice and you're ready for anything. I ate about three and was ready for a nap.

CAKES

BANANA CAKE

1. Preheat oven to 350 degrees. Line a muffin pan with 12 cupcake liners.

OR

Preheat oven to 350 degrees. Trace a 9-inch round cake pan on parchment paper with a pencil. Cut the circle out. Coat the cake pan with nonstick spray and flour and place parchment paper circle on top.

2. In a blender, mix a banana on medium speed until smooth and liquidy.

3. Sift the flour, baking soda, baking powder, sugar, and salt in a medium sized bowl.

4. In a separate bowl, whisk together the butter, banana, soymilk, and extracts.

5. Add the wet ingredients to the dry ingredients and stir with a rubber spatula until just combined. Fold in the chocolate chips and walnuts.

6. Using an ice cream scooper, fill cupcake liners about ⅔ of the way full. Bake for 18 minutes or until knife comes out clean. Transfer to cooling rack. Frost cupcakes when completely cooled.

 OR

Bake cake for 25 minutes or until a toothpick comes out clean when poked in the center of the cake.

7. To take the cake out, place a cooling rack on top of cake so the tiny legs are sticking up and not towards the cake, then flip the cooling rack and pan altogether, place on a surface, and remove the cake pan and parchment paper, slowly. Allow to fully cool before frosting.

Banana cake:
1 ¼ cup all-purpose flour
1 cup sugar
½ cup soymilk
⅓ cup coconut milk
½ cup blended banana
  (use a very ripe banana)
½ cup v. butter, melted
1 ¼ teaspoon baking
  powder
¼ teaspoon baking soda
1 teaspoon banana
  extract
1 tablespoon vanilla
  extract
½ cup chocolate chips*
¾ cup walnuts, chopped

Makes 12 cupcakes or one 9-inch cake layer. Double recipe for complete cake!

MAPLE MILK PUDDING

1. In a medium saucepan, whisk together the sugar, cornstarch, and salt.

2. Whisk in the coconut milk and soymilk over medium heat.

3. Stir constantly until the mixture is thick and pudding-like. Turn off heat and whisk in vanilla extract, maple extract, and butter until combined.

4. Transfer to a bowl and put plastic wrap directly on the entire surface of pudding. This prevents pudding skin from forming. Store in refrigerator.

CARAMELIZED CORN FLAKES

1. Preheat oven to 400 degrees. Line a baking sheet with parchment paper.

2. In a large bowl, carefully toss the corn flakes with the brown sugar, ¼ cup cornmeal, flour, and butter.

3. Spread the corn flakes evenly on the baking pan and dust remaining cornmeal over them.

4. Bake for about 5 minutes, stirring every once in awhile to ensure they cook evenly.

5. Take tray out, stir up the flakes, and let them sit on the baking pan to harden up more. When completely cooled and hardened, store them in a zip-lock bag.

Maple milk pudding:
⅓ cup sugar
¾ cup soymilk
¾ cup canned coconut milk
2 tablespoon + 2 teaspoon cornstarch
⅛ teaspoon salt
1 teaspoon butter
1 teaspoon vanilla extract
1 ½ teaspoon maple extract

Caramelized corn flakes:
2 cup corn flakes
½ cup maple syrup
⅓ cup v. butter, melted
¼ cup cornmeal + 2 tablespoon for dusting
¼ cup all-purpose flour

MAPLE FROSTING

1. Using an electric mixer with the whisk attachment, blend the butter and shortening together until light and creamy, on medium speed.

2. Add the maple syrup. Mix until it's well incorporated. Scrape the sides really well.

3. Add the powdered sugar until thoroughly mixed.

4. Add in the vanilla extract, and if using, the maple extract and blend on high speed. Mix until light and fluffy. The maple syrup in this may cause the frosting to melt faster, so make sure to keep refrigerated.

Cakes are cooled! Pudding is chilled! Frosting is whipped! S'gooooo!

When you're happy with your frosting job, sprinkle caramelizes cornflakes all over the whole cake. You might have to use two hands to get them to stick to the sides. It all comes together in the end, I promise!

Maple frosting:
½ cup shortening
½ cup v. butter
2 cup powdered sugar
¼ cup maple syrup
1 teaspoon maple extract (optional)
1 tablespoon vanilla extract

Makes enough frosting for 12 cupcakes or one 9-inch cake layer. Double recipe for 2-layer cake.

Growing up around and in LA, you grow accustomed to seeing those big plastic jugs with iced horchata among a bunch of other colorful juices and lemonades on the street, at restaurants, at farmers' markets, etc. There are many different variations of horchata, some naturally vegan, some not.

I love this horchata cake because you can get away with eating it for breakfast. It's like a heartier, more delicious Cinnamon Toast Crunch!

A heads up, if you wanna make this cake, plan ahead. When making homemade horchata, you have to soak the rice overnight.

HORCHATA CAKE

HORCHATA

1. Mix together the rice and water in a big bowl. Cover and let soak overnight.

2. Blend the water and rice on high for about 3 minutes. The rice should be really blended. The grain won't go away completely, but for the most part it should be gone.

3. Pour into a large bowl and mix in the soymilk and sugar until completely combined. Keep refrigerated.

Horchata:
1 cup white rice
2 cup water
4 teaspoon cinnamon
¼ cup sugar
2 cup soymilk

Double to make enough horchata for a complete cake.

Horchata cake:
1 cup horchata (see above)
½ tablespoon coconut vinegar
1 ¼ cup all-purpose flour
½ cup canola oil
½ tablespoon vanilla extract
¼ teaspoon salt
¼ teaspoon baking soda
½ tablespoon baking powder
⅔ cup sugar

Makes 12 cupcakes or one 9-inch cake layer. Double recipe for complete cake!

HORCHATA CAKE

1. Preheat oven to 350 degrees. Line a muffin pan with 12 cupcake liners.

OR

Preheat oven to 350 degrees. Trace a 9-inch round cake pan on parchment paper with a pencil. Cut the circle out. Coat the cake pan with nonstick spray and flour and place parchment paper circle on top.

2. In a large mixing bowl, whisk together the horchata and coconut vinegar. Set aside.

3. In a medium mixing bowl, sift flour, salt, baking soda, and baking powder together.

4. Once the horchata and vinegar have curdled for at least three minutes, add the oil, sugar, and vanilla to the mixture. Whisk until frothy. Slowly add the dry ingredients to the wet and mix until only small bumps remain.

5. Using an ice cream scooper, fill cupcake liners about two thirds of the way full. Bake for 18 minutes or until toothpick comes out clean.

OR

5. Bake cake for 25 minutes or until a toothpick comes out clean when poked in the center of the cake.

6. To take the cake out, place a cooling rack on top of cake so the tiny legs are sticking up and not towards the cake, then flip the cooling rack and pan altogether, place on a surface, and remove the cake pan and parchment paper, slowly. Allow to fully cool before frosting.

PUDDING

1. In a medium saucepan stir the sugar, cornstarch, and salt together. Whisk in the horchata over medium heat, stirring constantly until mixture is thick and pudding-like.

2. Remove from heat and stir in butter and vanilla.

3. Transfer pudding to a bowl and cover with plastic wrap directly on the surface of the pudding. Store in refrigerator.

FROSTING

1. In an electric mixer, cream together the butter and shortening on medium speed. Blend until completely creamy, making sure to scrape down the sides of the bowl.

2. Add in powdered sugar, horchata, and vanilla. Mix on highest speed, again, taking breaks to scrape down the sides of the bowl. Blend until smooth and light.

Horchata pudding:
1 ½ cup horchata (see opposite)
⅓ cup sugar
2 tablespoon + 2 teaspoon cornstarch
1 teaspoon v. butter
1 teaspoon vanilla extract
⅛ teaspoon salt

Horchata frosting:
½ cup v. butter
½ cup shortening
2 cup powdered sugar
¼ cup horchata (see opposite)
1 teaspoon vanilla extract

Makes enough frosting for 12 cupcakes or one 9-inch cake layer. Double recipe for 2-layer cake.

NEAPOLITAN CAKE

Neapolitan has a very special, goofy, place in my heart. The creation of this cake goes a little like this: In the seventh grade, I entered a vegan cupcake competition with my best friend Sophia. We were baking, but probably mainly dancing ridiculously like we do when we're together, and none of the cupcakes we made seemed special enough to be a winner. I'm not sure what really came over us, but we threw all these flavors around, and through our impeccable, soul-sister synergy, we came up with the Neapolitan cake. Ya girls' won too.

VANILLA CAKE

Vanilla cake:

1 ¼ cup all-purpose flour

¾ cup sugar

½ cup coconut milk

½ cup soymilk

½ cup v. butter

1 tablespoon coconut vinegar

½ tablespoon baking powder

2 teaspoon vanilla extract

Makes 12 cupcakes or one 9-inch cake layer. Double recipe for complete cake!

1. Preheat oven to 350 degrees. Line a muffin pan with 12 cupcake liners or trace a 9-inch round cake pan on parchment paper with a pencil. Cut the circle out. Coat the cake pan with nonstick spray and flour and place parchment paper circle on top.

2. Whisk the coconut milk, soymilk, and vinegar together until slightly foamy. Set aside.

3. While the milk and vinegar mixture is curdling, cream together the butter and sugar in an electric mixer using the whisk attachment. Mix on medium speed until light and fluffy. Scrape down sides of the bowl every once in awhile. Sugar granules will still remain, but that's okay.

4. Add vanilla extract to the butter and sugar and mix until it's fully incorporated.

5. In a separate bowl, sift the flour and baking powder together.

6. Gradually add in the flour mixture and the milk mixture to the butter-sugar mixture. Mix everything until smooth. Make sure that you scrape any buttery chunks you see into the middle of the bowl so you can smooth that sucker out.

7. Using an ice cream scoop, scoop batter into cupcake liners.

OR

If using a cake pan, pour batter into pan. Scrape all the batter out of the bowl using a rubber spatula. Even out the batter by

moving the pan back and forth.

8. Bake cupcakes 18 minutes or until toothpick comes out clean when poked in a cupcake. Transfer to cooling rack.

OR

Bake cake for 25 minutes or until a toothpick comes out clean when poked in the center of the cake.

9. To take the cake out, place a cooling rack on top of cake so the tiny legs are sticking up and not towards the cake, then flip the cooling rack and pan altogether, place on a surface, and remove the cake pan and parchment paper, slowly. Allow to fully cool before frosting.

CHOCOLATE PUDDING

Chocolate pudding:
⅓ cup cocoa powder
⅓ cup sugar
¾ cup coconut milk
¾ cup soymilk
2 tablespoon + 2
  teaspoon cornstarch
⅛ teaspoon salt
1 teaspoon v. butter

1. In a medium saucepan, whisk together the cocoa powder, sugar, salt, and cornstarch.

2. On medium heat, whisk in the milks and stir constantly until thickened to pudding consistency.

3. Remove from heat and whisk in vanilla extract and butter.

4. Place a sheet of plastic wrap directly on surface of pudding to prevent a skin from forming. Refrigerate until ready to serve.

NEAPOLITAN CAKE

CAKES

STRAWBERRY FROSTING

1. Using an electric mixer with the whisk attachment on medium speed, cream together the shortening and butter.

2. Add in powdered sugar, soymilk, strawberry extract, vanilla extract, and red food coloring. Mix on medium, then crank it up all the way to high to mix out any graininess. Add soymilk about a teaspoon at a time and speed up if it's too thick or grainy.

Strawberry frosting:
½ cup v. butter
½ cup shortening
2-2 ½ cup powdered
  sugar
2-3 tablespoon soymilk
1 teaspoon vanilla extract
1 teaspoon strawberry
  extract
2 drops red food coloring

Makes enough frosting for 12 cupcakes or one 9-inch cake layer. Double recipe for 2-layer cake.

SAMOA CAKE

I became vegan before I ever tried a Samoas Girl Scout Cookie. I was too freaked out by coconut at the time so I stuck with Thin Mints. I've made countless coconut, caramel, chocolatey cupcakes without knowing they were technically Samoas cakes. I think this cake is deserving of the "Girl Scout Gold Award."

COCONUT CAKE

1. Preheat oven to 350 degrees. Line a muffin pan with 12 cupcake liners.

OR

Preheat oven to 350 degrees. Trace a 9-inch round cake pan on parchment paper with a pencil. Cut the circle out. Coat the cake pan with nonstick spray and flour and place parchment paper circle on top.

2. In a large mixing bowl, whisk together the coconut milk and vinegar until foamy. Set aside while preparing the next steps.

3. In a medium mixing bowl, sift together the flour, baking powder, baking soda, and salt.

4. Using an electric mixer, mix the butter, coconut oil, and sugar on medium speed until light and fluffy.

5. Add vanilla extract to the butter and sugar mixture.

6. Add the dry ingredients and the coconut milk-vinegar to the butter. Mix on medium speed until no large clumps remain. Mix in the coconut flakes.

7. Using an ice cream scooper, fill cupcake liners about ⅔ of the way full. Bake for 18 minutes or until knife comes out clean. Transfer to cooling rack. Frost cupcakes when completely cooled.

Coconut cake:
1 cup canned coconut milk
1 ¼ cup all-purpose flour
1 cup toasted coconut flakes
¼ cup melted coconut oil
¼ cup v. butter at room temperature
¾ cup sugar
2 teaspoon vanilla extract
½ tablespoon coconut vinegar
1 tablespoon baking powder
1 teaspoon baking soda
¼ teaspoon salt

Makes 12 cupcakes or one 9-inch cake layer. Double recipe for complete cake!

OR

Bake cake for 25 minutes or until a toothpick comes out clean when poked in the center of the cake.

8. To take the cake out, place a cooling rack on top of cake so the tiny legs are sticking up and not towards the cake, then flip the cooling rack and pan altogether, place on a surface, and remove the cake pan and parchment paper, slowly. Allow to fully cool before frosting.

SAMOA FROSTING

Samoa frosting:
2 ½ cup toasted, flaked coconut
1 cup brown sugar
½ cup coconut milk
¾ cup soymilk
½ tablespoon vanilla extract
3 tablespoon cornstarch
½ teaspoon salt

Makes enough frosting for 12 cupcakes or one 9-inch cake layer. Double recipe for 2-layer cake.

1. In a small bowl, whisk together the soymilk and cornstarch. Set aside.

2. In a medium saucepan over medium heat, whisk the brown sugar into the coconut milk until the mixture boils. Lower the temperature and cook for 5 minutes, it should thicken.

3. Add the soymilk and cornstarch and salt slowly to the brown sugar-milk mixture on low heat, stirring constantly until the mixture is very thick. Turn off heat and add in the vanilla until completely mixed in. Stir in the toasted coconut. Store in refrigerator and allow to cool before using.

CHOCOLATE SAUCE

Chocolate sauce:
¼ cup soymilk
1 cup bitter-sweet chocolate chips*
1 tablespoon v. butter

1. In a small saucepan, cook soymilk until it just starts to boil.

2. Turn off heat and whisk chocolate chips in until totally smooth. Stir in butter.

CAKES

SAMOA CAKE

Sexy cake was created in preparation for my first year selling at Los Angeles Vegan Food & Beer Festival, now called Eat Drink Vegan. I needed to make a dessert that would pair well with all kinds of beer. My answer to that was tangy, sweet lime cake with a spicy, salty blueberry filling and lime frosting with a swirl of the blueberry filling. It satisfies all your taste buds at once, hence *sexy*.

LIME CAKE

1. Preheat oven to 350 degrees. Line a muffin pan with 12 cupcake liners.

OR

Preheat oven to 350 degrees. Trace a 9-inch round cake pan on parchment paper with a pencil. Cut the circle out. Coat the cake pan with nonstick spray and flour and place parchment paper circle on top.

Lime cake:

1 ¼ cup all-purpose flour
1 teaspoon baking powder
½ teaspoon baking soda
⅓ cup soymilk
½ cup melted v. butter
½ tablespoon coconut vinegar
¾ cup sugar
1 teaspoon vanilla extract
¼ cup lime juice
i teaspoon lime zest

Makes 12 cupcakes or one 9-inch cake layer. Double recipe for complete cake!

2. In a measuring cup, whisk together the soymilk and coconut vinegar. Set aside and allow to curdle for a few minutes.

3. In a medium mixing bowl, sift the flour, baking soda, and baking powder together.

4. Using an electric mixer with the whisk attachment, cream together the butter and sugar.

5. Add the vanilla extract, lime juice, and lime zest to the butter and sugar mixture on medium speed until well incorporated.

6. Slowly add in the dry ingredients and the buttermilk mixture to the wet ingredients. Mix on medium speed until batter is smooth.

7. Line a muffin pan with twelve cupcake liners. Using an ice cream scooper, fill cupcake liners about ⅔ of the way full. Bake for 18 minutes or until a toothpick comes out clean. Transfer to cooling rack. Frost cupcakes when completely cooled.

OR

Bake cake for 25 minutes or until a toothpick comes out clean when poked in the center of the cake.

8. To take the cake out, place a cooling rack on top of cake so the tiny legs are sticking up and not towards the cake, then flip the cooling rack and pan altogether, place on a surface, and remove the cake pan and parchment paper, slowly. Allow to fully cool before frosting.

SEXY SAUCE

1. In a medium saucepan, gently combine the blueberries, sugar, key lime juice, cayenne pepper, salt, and lime zest. Allow to simmer for an hour on medium to low heat, stirring every now and then.

2. When mixture has thickened, remove from heat and store in refrigerator.

SEXY FROSTING

1. Using an electric mixer with the whisk attachment, on medium speed, blend the butter and shortening together until light and creamy.

2. Add the powdered sugar and key lime juice. Mix on medium speed until it's well incorporated. Scrape the sides really well.

3. Add in the vanilla extract, blend on high speed. The frosting should become light about a minute in. Using a spatula, gently fold in the sexy sauce.

Sexy sauce:
1 container fresh blueberries
¼ cup sugar
½ cup key lime juice
¼ teaspoon cayenne pepper
½ teaspoon salt
zest of 1 key lime

Sexy frosting:
½ cup shortening
½ cup v. butter
2 ½ cup powdered sugar
4 tablespoon key lime juice
1 teaspoon vanilla extract
¼ cup sexy sauce

Makes enough frosting for 12 cupcakes or one 9-inch cake layer. Double recipe for 2-layer cake.

MY KITCHEN MY CLUB

I feel like I've become an avid dancer because of the amount of time I spend in the kitchen. When I'm alone, baking for hours, the kitchen becomes my dance club. I wanna bake to fast, groovy songs that make every stir feel like a part of a dance move.

Here are some songs that never fail to get me in the groove of baking and doing dishes:

"Temperature" — Sean Paul
"Get Right" — Jennifer Lopez
"Don't Fight It, Feel It" — Primal Scream
"Down On My Luck" — Vic Mensa
"Maneater" — Nelly Furtado
"These Walls" — Kendrick Lamar
"I'm Not Dancing" — Tirzah
"Tomboy" — Princess Nokia
"Got It Good" — Kaytranada
"Groove Is in the Heart" — Deee-Lite
"Lady (Hear Me Tonight)" — Modjo
"Return of the Mack" — Mark Morrison

claracakes.com

GEAR

The gear I use every day to bake is very typical kitchen equipment. I've never attended a culinary school, so I'm a bit clueless as to what equipment and tools I technically *should* have. That being said, I've loved each and every one of the following tools and could not do my baking without them.

KitchenAid Mixer: When I started baking, I used my great-great-aunt's 50-year-old, mint-green KitchenAid mixer that had been passed down in the family. It worked like new. I now use a Professional 600 Series 6-Quart KitchenAid. I love to pretend that I'm driving a sports car when I turn the speed to the highest level. Maybe that's the secret to the lightest frosting?

If you don't have a stand mixer, you can get away with hand whisking and mixing batters and doughs. I recommend using vegan butter at room temperature so that it's easier to incorporate into the other ingredients. You may have to work a little harder, but you might as well start working off those cookie calories now!

Frosting is a bit more tricky. Unfortunately, an electric mixer blended frosting always comes out better than a hand whisked frosting. You need to whisk the shortening and butter for a good while in order to break both ingredients down to become one creamy frosting base. It's also crucial to break down powdered sugar clumps with an electric mixer, otherwise you'll have grainy frosting. If you don't have a stand mixer, I highly recommend using a hand mixer. It's less fuss than a stand electric mixer and much more affordable, but will get the job done just as nicely.

Food Processor: I didn't buy a food processor until recently, when I started to cook more. Now that I have it, I love it. It's great for making cookie crusts, especially grinding up cereal. I still prefer making old-school pie dough with my hands, though. I use a 12-cup Cuisinart.

"Sifter": When I first started baking I went out and bought a sifter and threw it away pretty quickly after. They rust easily and are super hard to clean. Instead, I use a circular pasta strainer (preferably one that is all mesh) and hook it onto a medium sized bowl. It's punk. It's easier to clean.

Whisk: You can't do much without a whisk. A whisk—combined with the speed of your hand—evenly combines ingredients. Don't buy a flimsy rubber one, buy a stealth, stainless steel one.

Rubber Spatulas: Rubber spatulas are key for scraping bowls, folding in ingredients, and stirring batters together that are to not be over-mixed. They're also perfect for rewarding yourself and licking the batter.

Mixing Bowls: I like to use metal mixing bowls because my hands are much too clumsy for glass bowls. I keep a lot of mixing bowls on hand so if I'm on a roll I don't have to continuously wash one or two.

Baking Sheets: Baking Sheets are a must for baking cookies and toasting nuts and coconut flakes.

Cake Pans: Get some nice 9-inch round cake pans, and make sure to get two! That way when you're making a layered cake you're cooking both layers at the same time.

Grease Proof Cake Boards: Unless you're going to present your cake directly on a cake stand or plate, you'll need to place your cake on a cardboard cake board. Especially, if you're transporting the cake from one place to another.

Glass Casserole Pans: I love using glass casserole pans for bars because you can see the edges of the bars and figure out how much more oven time they need. Most of the recipes call for an 8x8 pan or a 9x13 pan.

Cooling Racks: Cooling racks are critical for completing the baking process. If you don't cool your cakes, cupcakes, pies, and cookies on them they'll become either soggy or too crunchy.

Pie Tins: I use 9-inch pie tins. Aluminum is great if you're gifting a pie to someone, but if you're looking to reuse yours I'd go with a steel or glass one. Glass if you want your pie to shine real bright.

Rolling Pin: You can't roll out pie dough without a rolling pin! I use a wooden one with handles on either side that my family has had for years and it works like a charm.

GEAR

Ice Cream Scoop: I don't know what I would do without my ice cream scoop for making cupcakes. I use the ice cream scoop to get the perfect amount of batter into each cupcake liner.

Parchment Paper: I use parchment paper for almost everything except cupcakes. Any pan I use for a whole cake, bars, or cookies gets lined with parchment paper. If you don't use parchment paper, there's a very high risk that whatever you're baking will stick to the pan.

Cupcake Liners: The fun part! I can spend hours online looking at all the cupcake liners out in the world. You can find just about any pattern out there. Step your cupcake game up and get some cute ones!

Mixer Attachments: In this cookbook you'll need the paddle attachment for cookies and doughs, and the whisk attachment for batters and frostings.

Spoons: Cuz you gotta taste!

Toothpicks: I use toothpicks to stick in the center of cakes and cupcakes to check if they come out clean. If they come out clean, they're done.

Measuring Spoons: You're gonna need measuring spoons for each of these recipes to ensure you add the exact right amount of each little ingredient, like baking powders, salt, spices, extracts, etc. You can never have too many of these

Measuring Cups: I prefer plastic measuring cups because they're easier to clean. I also like to use a glass measuring cup, especially if I need to heat something up in the microwave like butter. That way everything is measured and melted directly in that glass, saving you from having to wash another bowl.

Timer: This is essential so you will know the exact time you need to check on what's baking in the oven (if you're oven doesn't already have one built in).

Disposable Piping Bag: As much as I'd like to use reusable piping bags, they just get gross. They're very difficult to wash. I prefer plastic piping bags because you can toss them when you're done. I use piping bags for frosting and for filling cupcakes with puddings and sauces.

Wide, Plastic Drinking Cup: To fill my pastry bag with filling, I place the pastry bag in a plastic cup and pull the edges around the rim of the cup. It opens the bag up making it easy to place filling inside.

Frosting Tip 12: Wilton makes so many different frosting tips, but I use this one to stuff pudding or sauces into cupcakes with.

Butter Knife: I like to use a butter knife to swirl in sauces on the top of frosting on cupcakes.

Plastic Wrap: You will need plastic wrap to protect the surface of puddings and sauces you make, that way they won't form that weird outer skin. You will also need it to cover nuts that you soak overnight, to wrap around dough, and many, many other things.

Completely Metal Spatula: A sturdy metal spatula is key for lifting cookies off baking sheets in one swoop. It's also super handy to have on hand to scrape burned bits and pieces off the bottom of the oven in case you start smelling something burning!

Sauce Pan: You will need a sauce pan for sauces and puddings. I prefer a nonstick.

Silicon Pinch Mitts: I don't know the exact name for these but they're lifesavers. I don't like using towels or thick oven mitts to pull out hot dishes because they're not grippy enough. These silicon mitts are super grippy, and completely protect your hand from getting burned.

Airy Basketball Shorts: It's not fun to bake in constricting pants or shorts, especially when it's 100 degrees outside and your kitchen becomes a sweets sauna. My answer to that is basketball shorts. They dry fast wish is great for dish washing and they let your skin breathe. Whew!

Ugly Tee, Baggy Tee Shirts: I'd go nuts if I couldn't wipe my hands on my baking clothing. Each baking shirt I have is completely stained with cocoa powder, oil, food coloring, just about any messy ingredient there is.

Baking Socks: At home, I don't like baking barefoot, mainly because my feet get wet from doing the dishes and then they just start to feel dirty. I prefer baking in some ugly socks I don't care about. When in a commercial kitchen I prefer canvas Vans or rubber Klogs.

Hair Tie/Rubber Bands: Get that hair up and away from your batters and doughs! The last thing you want is a long hair baked in your beautiful cake.

GEAR

EGG, DAIRY, AND GELATIN SUBSTITUTES

This is the guide for the ingredients that substitute animal products, and for some that might be harder to find at supermarkets.

Egg Substitutes:

Coconut Vinegar: I use coconut vinegar mainly to create a buttermilk by mixing soymilk (and coconut milk sometimes) and vinegar together. It's also used in the s'mores bars recipe. I love it because the taste is mellow, and when combined with soymilk and coconut milk it's scent has the sorta tangy bite to it that dairy has. I can insure you that the vinegar bakes off, and you can't even taste it in batter. If you aren't able to find coconut vinegar, use apple cider vinegar just as you would use coconut vinegar.

Flaxseed Meal: If your old-school parent or relative or whoever catches you putting this brown, healthy looking stuff into brownies they're gonna question you so hard! Stash it, disguise it, sneak it in when they're not lookin', just do what you gotta do it to use it. I mainly use it for things like brownies and other bars because it binds the ingredients very similarly to what an egg might do.

Applesauce: Applesauce is definitely the most lighthearted egg replacer. It's such a staple snack that no one really bothers to question you for it. I use applesauce in cookies because it keeps the color light, and you don't see any tiny brown flaxseed meal in what should be a completely golden chocolate chip cookie. It has a similar wetness that eggs would have which you want for a cookie recipe.

Banana: You might notice in the Banana Cake recipe in this book, I don't use any vinegar. This is because bananas are the perfect egg substitute. Banana sorta soaks up all the ingredients and binds them into a delicious cake. I recommend using bananas as an egg substitute only when making banana flavored baked goods. Otherwise, it'll add an unnecessary banana flavor.

Mori-Nu Extra Firm Silken Tofu*: Please, save yourself some time, order one or two online so that you always have em in your arsenal. Most supermarkets won't carry this ingredient. I use this tofu for the pies because when blended its perfectly creamy and holds its body well. There's no obvious tofu texture or taste with it. It's really inexpensive and you don't have to store it in the fridge (before opened).

Ener-G Egg Replacer*: I really try to limit my use of this since I think it makes a lot of desserts chalky, but for some reason it does the trick for the potato chip blondies. No chalkiness, all deliciousness. This a health food store or online purchase.

Gelatin Substitute:

Agar Powder*: Agar powder (or agar-agar) is a naturally occurring gelling agent that comes from seaweed. It has no taste or color. Agar powder helps cream pies hold their structure. It's always heartbreaking when you slice a pie you poured your heart into, only for it to just run out like pudding on crust. Just like Mori-Nu Tofu, you wanna have this in your arsenal to save you a last minute health food store trip. It's nearly impossible to find agar in powder form even at health food stores, so deeeefinitely buy online!

Milk Substitutes:

Coconut Milk: I prefer to use canned coconut milk because it's creamier than cartons of refrigerated coconut milk. Coconut milk has a very similar consistency to that of cream. When refrigerated for a few hours, the fat rises to the top of the can, which you can use as an instant cream replacement. I use coconut milk with soymilk in cakes. That way the coconut milk provides the fluffiness, and the soymilk holds everything together while also making a smoother batter. I also use coconut milk in puddings and pies since it provides a perfect creamy texture. If you're not a coconut person, swap it out for more soymilk. In my opinion, the coconut flavor cooks off, especially since I typically combine it with soymilk.

Shake it up real well before using. Coconut milk's consistency is completely susceptible to the weather outside. So, if it's cold out, heat the milk up for a couple minutes until it melts a bit. Stir really well, then resume. It might be easier just to buy a carton of coconut milk, but it's way runnier, and results in less fluffy cakes than if using canned coconut milk.

Soymilk: Soymilk is by far my favorite non-dairy milk. Almond milk is delicious tasting, but it just doesn't bake, blend, or hold puddings together like soymilk. Soymilk's consistency is perfect, the flavor bakes/cooks off, and the fat holds everything together so nicely.

Vegan Butter Substitutes:

Butter: The Earth Balance vegan butter brand is my go-to butter for everything I make. It's sold at most supermarkets, and definitely Whole Foods, Sprouts, and other health food stores. If you can't find it there, there's always Amazon. Traditionally, most pastry chefs use unsalted butter as a way to control the salt level in pastries. There's no unsalted vegan butter on the market that I'm aware of, so, in many of these recipes I don't call for salt.

Coconut Oil: Coconut oil can be used as a delicious substitute for butter in things like shortbreads and cookies. I wouldn't recommend swapping it for butter in frosting because it'll melt at room temperature.

Vegan Cream Substitutes:

Cream Cheese*: I use cream cheese in a couple pies. My preferred brand is Follow Your Heart. Before they had their line of amazing vegan products like Vegenaise, they started out with the Follow Your Heart Market & Cafe in the valley. It still feels like a vegetarian restaurant from the 70s. Anyway, their cream cheese tastes and works just like dairy cream cheese. If you can't find vegan cream cheese at the store, use extra lemon to get that tangy flavor.

Whipped Cream*: I love SO Delicious' tub whipped cream. You can buy it in the frozen section of health food stores and possibly some supermarkets. I use the whipped cream to top cream pies and, in some cases, to mix into pie ingredients. Just make sure you let it thaw out in the refrigerator a few hours before using.

Cashews: I use whole, raw, unsalted cashews for homemade ricotta and pies. You have to leave them in water overnight so that the cashews soak up the liquid and become creamy when blended. If you skip that step, your pie will be very grainy.

Almonds: I use raw, slivered almonds to make homemade ricotta which I use for the chocolate ricotta cheesecake. Like cashews, you need to soak them overnight for them to achieve a creamy texture.

Marshmallow Substitute:

I use **Dandies Marshmallows.*** They're my favorite marshmallows by far and are run by a vegan company based out of Chicago called Chicago Vegan Foods who also manufacture Teese Vegan Cheese and Temptation Vegan Ice Cream. Dandies taste even better than the gelatin filled ones!

Chocolate Chips:

Chocolate Chips*: I use only semi-sweet chocolate chips in this book. You can find vegan semi-sweet chocolate chips at COSTCO, or from brands such as Enjoy Life, Trader Joe's, and Guittard.

White Chocolate Chips*: I love using white chocolate chips in winter recipes to balance out delicious spices. I buy chocolate chips from King David on Amazon.

INGREDIENTS GUIDE

AKA "I just wanna put this all on the table....."

If you're like me, you won't read this. If you're smart, you'll read this and won't make half the mistakes I did when using and buying these ingredients!

In addition to the vegan substitutes listed in the previous section, these are all the other components needed to make magic. For each ingredient I listed I tried to be as PC as possible. So, organic, hopefully certified-vegan, non-GMO, etc. If you're ballin' on a budget, I won't judge you for buying non-certified, politically incorrect stuff. You're already making me so proud baking vegan!

Flour: Unbleached all-purpose flour will do ya just fine in all of these recipes. I don't know what else to tell you about it—it's a staple! These recipes are not trying to be healthy. Indulge.

Sugars:

Granulated Sugar: I use granulated sugar in just about everything. When you're at the market in the sugar section, look for sugar that is more beige than pure white. I avoid the bright white sugar because animal bone char is often used in the processing. I prefer the Zulka brand. It's inexpensive and works just like the bleached sugar.

Brown Sugar: You can either buy the expensive organic brown sugar, which saves some cleaning time, or you can make your own brown sugar. It's as simple as adding one tablespoon of molasses per cup of granulated sugar.

Maple Syrup: I'm not very fancy when it comes to maple syrup. When you were raised dunking all your frozen pancakes and waffles into Login Cabin, you don't grow up to be too much of a syrup snob. I buy whatever maple syrup is on sale. I love using maple syrup for last-minute sugar adjustments to cream pies since adding a granulated sugar would introduce coarse sugar granules in what should otherwise be a smooth pie.

Cocoa Powder: The higher quality the cocoa powder you use, the richer the flavor, the darker the color. What you pay for is what you get. Cocoa powder is pricey, so I understand whatever choice you make. Have you ever spilled a whole container of cocoa powder on the floor and had to vacuum then mop it up? I have. Open package carefully, over the sink, and when you're done using it put the darn lid back on.

Oils, Nut-Butter, Shortenings:

Peanut Butter: I always use peanut butter that's advertised as smooth and natural. I, preferably, buy the "no-stir" kind since I still haven't figured out how to stir peanut butter without the top layer of oil spilling out right onto me.

Canola Oil: When I want a lighter cake, I use canola oil, and plenty of it. It can seem intimidating at first, but don't be scared of it. It's what makes these cakes moist and the opposite of the dry "cardboard-like" vegan cake stereotype.

Shortening: I have a love-hate relationship with shortening. I hate how the only way to completely wash it off my hands and dishes is with lots of soap and hot, hot water. I love it because it's what makes these frosting recipes so smooooth and helps the inception cookie dough be so pliable. Make sure to buy all-vegetable shortening (duh).

Thickeners:

Cornstarch: I use cornstarch in the puddings and fruit sauces. Cornstarch is a wonderful thickener as long as you mix it with other dry ingredients before mixing the wet in, or when you mix it with a liquid really well, then slowly add to the sauce you're making. The last thing you want is for big, weird, powdery clumps of cornstarch to ruin your hard work.

Baking Powder, Baking Soda: Sounds similar, but do not confuse the two. I've had a few batches of cookies made with baking powder instead of baking soda come out really doughy and weird. Dedicate a baking soda just for baking, and dedicate one for making your fridge not smell gross because you definitely don't want to add smelly baking soda to a vanilla cake.

Extracts:

Vanilla Extract: The higher the price, the more refined the flavor. If you're going for the affordable one, add a little extra to the recipe. If you're an avid baker, it's smart to invest in a large bottle, otherwise you're gonna be running to the market all the time for an expensive, tiny bottle.

Maple Extract: If you can enhance a flavor, why not? This is definitely an online purchase, unless you have a cake and candy supply shop near you.

Strawberry Extract: I grew up eating Betty Crocker strawberry frosting out of the tub. I want my homemade strawberry frosting to have that rich strawberry flavor. I used to crush up fresh strawberries and add it to vanilla frosting, but it made the frosting too watery and the flavor wasn't strong enough. Strawberry extract saved the day. Get this at your local cake and candy supply shop, or online.

Banana Extract: I only recently started using banana extract, but now I'm hooked. As long as you use a small amount, it heightens the banana flavor beautifully. You can find this at most supermarkets.

Cereal, Graham Crackers, Rice, Cornmeal:

Cap'n Crunch: I use Cap'n Crunch mainly for the Butterfinger pie recipe. When crushed, then mixed with peanut butter, it tastes just like the crispy cookie inside a Butterfinger. I also always love a good bowl of Cap'n Crunch.

Cornflakes: Cornflakes go in the breakfast cake. I'd buy the organic kind, if possible. You can put this stuff in a bowl with a bunch of soymilk and eat it for breakfast, too! Who knew!

Graham Crackers: I use Nabisco Grahams. For some amazing reason, these do not have honey in them and are completely vegan. Only use them fresh, they're bland and soft when stale.

Oreos: Believe it or not, Oreos are vegan by default here in the United States. Don't ask me how, just enjoy. If you're in another country, watch out. A lot of international Oreos contain whey or gelatin.

Cornmeal: I use white cornmeal in some fruit bar crusts and in the chocolate ricotta pie. Although an unexpected pairing, cornmeal completely heightens the flavors of fruit, coconut, and chocolate.

Nonstick Cooking Spray: You can find coconut oil cooking spray at most markets. Just check the labels to be sure they're all clear of animal ingredients.

SWEETS ON THE GO

A lot of the times when we bake, we're baking for an event, party, potluck, or show. The thing all these have in common? They're not at our house! Transporting desserts from place to place can be tricky, but here are some tips that can help you out.

Plan your baking time so that cakes and cupcakes are able to be in the refrigerator for a couple hours. This makes the frosting more sturdy and less likely to get smeared easily.

Invest in a plastic cake container. You can find some nice, affordable ones online. I'd go with a 12-inch round cake container, as long as you're using a 12-inch cake board. That way, the cake has no way of sliding around.

Use a plastic cupcake container. As much as I love the classic pink cake boxes, cupcakes slide around in there unless they're completely packed in. You can buy containers that are literally made for cupcakes. You just pack each cupcake into their spot on the tray. They're perfectly spaced out for you, so you don't have to worry about frostings getting on each other.

So you have containers, but your work is still not done here. You must **pack the container tightly** in the car, so that is has no way of sliding around. I always keep a reusable bag with a coin purse inside to put next to cupcake containers. Basically, you wanna create a sturdy border around the container.

Bars are much easier to transport. You can wrap foil over the top and call it a day. I'd wait to cut the bars until you're at the event to ensure freshness and reduce crumbs.

I still haven't quite figured out how to transport cookies without smearing the chocolate chips. I **pack cookies in large plastic bags,** make sure to let all the air out, and seal them. Cookies do best in plastic bags because it allows for their moisture to be retained. They'll get stale very quickly if they're boxed up for a day or two. Air tight is key!

Pies aren't too tricky to pack up, either. I prefer using pie tins that are sold with plastic lids at the market. When I can't find those, I use foil and try to balloon it over the pie so I don't ruin the surface of the pie.

Blast the AC, make your turns carefully, and you should be good to go!

ACKNOWLEDGEMENTS

To my Mom. Your insight on every question I've had is truly the backbone of this book. You mean the world to me.

To my family. Andy, I wouldn't have started selling at shows if it weren't for you. Thank you for coming to my events to help out. As much as I might roll my eyes in the moment, your jokes lift everyone's spirits up. Thank you Dad for instilling a strong work ethic and a huge sweet tooth in me. To my brother Tyler for your help at events and making each customer laugh with your quick wit. Thank you Grandma for coming out to some very gnarly events like FYF and helping us sling mac and cheese waffles.

To Carol Glasser for showing me the ropes of how to pipe frosting when I was in seventh grade and just starting out.

To Jim Smith of The Smell for providing a home away from home where I was able to present my hobby to an entirely new crowd of people.

To quarrygirl for writing about my desserts resulting in many customers. For making cooking videos with me, and so graciously giving me your feedback.

To Salman Agah and Price Latimer of Pizzanista for giving my cupcakes a daily spot in your restaurant and for your business expertise and overall life inspiration.

To Ed and Deanna Templeton for spreading the word about my desserts and latest projects when I was just starting out.

To Kezia and Gary for hustling my first TV appearance out of the kindness of your heart.

To Alicia Pell for your advice and helping me understand confusing legal talk.

To Julie Gueraseva of *LAIKA* magazine for giving me my first cover shoot and constant support.

To Laura, Jonathan, Cynthia, and Jenn at Thank You For Coming for letting me pretend to have a diner in your restaurant for a couple days and for all your help.

To Sean Carlson for having me set up shop at FYF Presents shows and FYF Festival.

To Patrick O'Dell for featuring me in Vans' "Living Off The Wall" video series which led to many more opportunities.

To Michelle de Leon for our nights out dancing, pep talks, and incredible friendship.

To Abrielle Lopez for your sunshine and optimism and knowing me inside and out.

To Sophia Longo for your sisterhood, your advice, your love, and your haikus. You know me better than I do sometimes.

To Graeme Flegenheimer for having me cater your punk fests each summer, before I had even embarked on cooking savory food.

To my amazing customers. Thank you for coming out to each pop-up shop, ordering your birthday cakes and treats from me, and words of encouragement. If I didn't have a support system like you, it would be a lot harder to believe in myself.

Written in memory of Molly Anderson and Piper Goldstein. Two strong, fearless women who both individually influenced me and my business and continue to inspire me to this day.

Molly, when I was a freshman in high school, I remember you leading me into the kitchen of you and your husband's gourmet vegan restaurant, Madeleine Bistro, and letting me see how the kitchen worked. Madeleine Bistro made a weekly "Bistro Box" that included specials, some of their classic dishes, and snacks that people could order each week. Molly rallied for my desserts to be featured in the boxes every week. For her to take my new business under Madeleine Bistro's established, upscale, wing, meant the world. Molly, you made me feel like anything was possible. That I could bake, I could cook, and I could do it all vegan, while having fun. I can't tell you how much I miss my mom and I delivering cupcakes to you every Monday and catching up.

Piper, your no BS attitude made me feel like I could express myself without apology. That I could fully back my business without a doubt. The first day I met you, you told me, "Cheaper is no longer in your vocabulary. From now on, you use the word inexpensive." If I catch myself saying cheaper, I still think of you. Thank you for texting me tips on how to get yeast to activate for donuts, thank you for letting me set up shop at your beautiful market, and thank you for making me feel like being a woman in the food industry can be a very powerful thing. Your presence alone changed my life.

Your spirits inspire me every day.

Published in the United States by powerHouse Books,
a division of powerHouse Cultural Entertainment, Inc.
37 Main Street, Brooklyn, NY 11201-1021
telephone 212.604.9074, fax 212.366.5247
e-mail: info@powerHouseBooks.com
website: www.powerHouseBooks.com

First edition, 2017

Library of Congress Control Number: 2016957328

Hardcover ISBN 978-1-57687-823-1

Printed by Toppan Leefung

Photographs by Logan White
Book design by Krzysztof Poluchowicz

10 9 8 7 6 5 4 3 2 1

Printed and bound in China